THE GOSPEL ACCORDING TO RUTH

A SEASON OF HARVEST
121 DAYS OF DEVOTIONS

A Daily Devotional

KEVIN FOSTER

Cover Illustration by Gustave Dore.
Cover design and editing services by Phil Wade, Brandywinebooks.net

ISBN: 978-1-942587-15-6

Published by Carpenter's Son Publishing, Franklin, Tennessee.

Carpenter's Son Publishing

DEDICATED TO THE LORD OF GLORY

"For he that is mighty hath done to me great things;
and holy is his name."
(Luke 1:49 KJV)

CONTENTS

LABOR OF THE SOUL

REST OF THE SOUL

MARRIAGE OF THE SOUL

Encouragement on My Journey

I want to thank all of the following people for their encouragement and spiritual, godly insights to me on my journey. Their ministry in my life is immeasurable.

Grandparents Pastor Henry and Vivian Culpepper, Sister Ruth Moon (Great Aunti), Brother Paul and Sister Madelyn Wiegmular, Brother Ed Bryant, Brother Dave Mitchell, Brother Michael Wootan, Sister Cooper, Sister Lois Balzer, Sister Dorothy Olson, Chaplain Tony and Sylvia Petrone, Brother Rick and Sister Rose Kelly, Brother Mike and Sister Georgia Sanders, Brother Tim and Sister Jackie, Brother Rick Love, Brother Frank Hankins, Sister Rhoda Savage, Sister Alice Callaghan, Brother H. H. Wright, MD, Sister Sheila Wright, Elder O.J. and Sister Benjamin, Brother W.C. and Sister Jones, The Star Light Family, Brother Wallace Pope, Brother Ruff Jones, Elder Billingsley, Sister Gladys Jackson, Brother Fred Alexander and family, Chaplain Izetta Jackson, Brother Jeff Jamerson, Brother Soloman Reeves, Brother John Arevalo, Sister Audrey Ward, Sister Elaine Paige, Brother Lance Mountain, Brother Christian Hosoi, Brother Steve Caballero, Brother Eddie Elguera, Brother Richard Sanchez, Brother Nerses Boyadjian, Brother Ernest Carlson, Brother Clark Culpepper (Uncle), Pastor Donald Wyatt and the Milo Terrace Family, Brother Saro and Sister Arda Davidian, ABBC Deaf Ministry, Deaf Pastor Brian Burgwin, assistant Deaf Pastor Jack Conley and the Puente Hill Deaf Ministry, Sister Dee and Muriel and the Grace Bible Deaf and Blind Ministry, Brother Andre Walton and the Friday Morning Bible Breakfast Family, Sister Rica Tinnin, Sister Linda Flinn, Sister Darlene Mulvihill, Sister Virginia Echols, Brother Young

Kim, MD, Sister Ola Olambiwonnu, Brother Charlie and Sister Joyce Cooper, Brother Bill and Sister Willa Mae Horton, Brother Albert and Sister Australia Horton Swift, Sister Amber- Jean Horton, Sister Shawn Johnson, Brother Marshall McClain, Sister "Neen-Neen" Janine McClain, Sister Izora Prentice, C.J. Poindexter, my pleasant mother, Henriola Johnson, and my wonderfully lovely wife, Lanya.

PREFACE

In the fall of 2012, I was burdened with a vile spirit of this world, which I had pacified for years. As it grew, I became more miserable within my inner man. But God, who knows the struggles of our hearts, gave me the power to completely sever myself from those things, freeing me from one of many struggles. Christ took my sinful load, bearing it as only He can. A revival sprang forth in my heart, new and vibrant as sprouts in a well-watered garden!

During early spring of 2013, I was reading the Old Testament book of Ruth, and the love of God revealed to me a seedling, planted in my soul, in the form of a fresh look at this wonderfully glorious book. Over the course of the year I would awake daily and glean fruits I had not seen in my previous readings of Ruth. Those thoughts, prayers, insights, and poems are all gathered here in one sheaf for you to experience.

It is my prayer that you in like manner would gather spiritual fruits and truths from this book and develop a love for the Word of God unto righteousness for your journey until that great harvest day dawns in your life.

Love,
Brother Kevin Foster

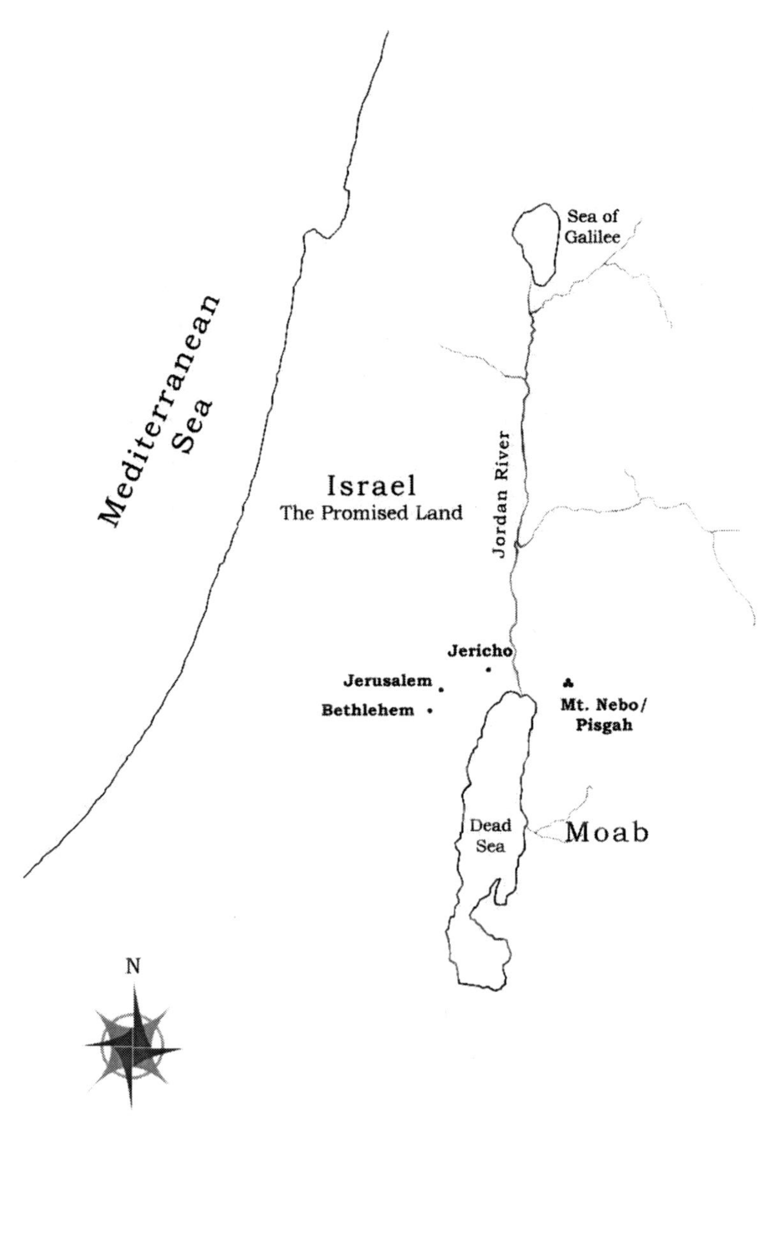
Sea of Galilee
Mediterranean Sea
Israel
The Promised Land
Jordan River
Jericho
Jerusalem
Bethlehem
Mt. Nebo/ Pisgah
Dead Sea
Moab
N

CALL
OF
THE
SOUL

1 Choose This Day Whom You Will Serve

"Now it came to pass, in the days when the judges ruled, that there was a famine in the land. And a certain man of Bethlehem, Judah, went to dwell in the country of Moab, he and his wife and his two sons." Ruth 1:1

Israel, the apple of God's eye, obtained glorious exploits over their enemies in the Promised Land, under the leadership of Joshua. Our Lord told Joshua, "No man shall be able to stand before you all the days of your life" (Joshua 1:5). There were setbacks as a result of their disobedience. However, when obeying God was their goal, they triumphed mightily. We all ought to make obeying God our goal in this brief life, following with humble hearts Jesus—our Joshua, our Savior.

Before his death Joshua exhorted the people, "And if it seems evil to you to serve the Lord, choose for yourselves this day whom you will serve, whether the gods which your fathers served that were on the other side of the River, or the gods of the Amorites, in whose land you dwell. But as for me and my house, we will serve the Lord" (Joshua 24:15). Stay on point. Stay the course. Keep your eyes fixed on the ways of God. He is our exceedingly great reward.

Sadly, after Joshua's death, the people began to sin against the Lord. "When all that generation had been gathered to their fathers, another generation arose after them who did not know the Lord nor the work which He had done for Israel. Then the children of Israel did evil in the sight of the Lord, and served the Baals; and they forsook the Lord God of their fathers…" (Judges 2:10–12).

Friends, serving the gods of the people around you cripples your walk with the true and living God. Serving other gods is more than bowing down before a lifeless relic or the worshiping of symbolic statutes. What are these other gods? Simply put, they are the things the world strives after, things that vie for mastery of your imagination and flesh. "Set your mind on things above, not on things on the earth" (Colossians 3:2). Whatever occupies your imagination occupies you.

"Do you not know that to whom you present yourselves slaves to obey, you are that one's slaves whom you obey, whether of sin leading to death, or of obedience leading to righteousness?" (Romans 6:16). Israel became enslaved to the enemies they were to conquer. Search your heart, dear friends. Have you become a slave to those things you've been called to conquer within the land of your heart, mind, and soul?

Pick of the Crop: Be not deceived—you're either serving God or the idols of this world. To whom are you bowing your heart? Are you serving God in the promises of His choosing or have you moved to Moab in the service of the gods of this world? Ask God to help you stay focused on Him and to serve Him only. The choice is yours.

2 Jesus Our Judge

"... in the days when the judges ruled..." Ruth 1:1

We're told the Lord had pity on His people and gave them judges to fight their enemies. "And it came to pass, when the judge was dead, that they reverted and behaved more corruptly than their fathers, by following other gods, to serve them and bow down to them. They did not cease from their own doings nor from their stubborn way" (Judges 2:19). This is God's endless love for His people that, while they were still in sin, He gave judges to rule, contend with, and defend them. These judges were ministers of God, His representatives.

"The Lord is not slack concerning His promise, as some count slackness, but is longsuffering toward us, not willing that any should perish but that all should come to repentance" (2 Peter 3:9). God gave His people judges for nearly 450 years (Acts 13:20). During those times, Israel would return in and out of a state of anarchy individually and as a nation. When there were no judges, every man did that which was right in his own eyes.

Israel was like a candle in its own wax whose wick was nearly spent. The people would flame into a blast of brightness when a judge ruled, only to have the glow stymied at the death of that judge. Is the Judge of all the earth ruling in our hearts? Is He? Or are we doing what is right in our own eyes?

Lawlessness awaits the person or nation when everyone does that which is right in their own eyes. That was our state of mind before coming to Christ. We judged ourselves by ourselves. We resisted the call of God in our lives. Pride and contention reigned within our souls.

We were literally warring against the love of God who holds the next beat of our hearts in His hand. Foolish rebels were we! But God sent the Judge of all the Earth to pardon and cleanse whosoever will. That Judge is Jesus.

Bethlehem means the "House of Bread." In our story, it's synonymous with salvation and staple, fullness and peace, joy, promise, life, increase, holiness, triumph, truth, jubilation, exultation, freedom, revelation, liberty, living, growth, and glee—the rule of law within the perfect will of God.

Moab is symbolic of sin, death and dying, devastation, destruction and doom, disease, mayhem, misery, an upheaval, havoc, disorder, disruption, a curse and bondage, living an immoral life within an imperfect world in rebellion against God. It's where those who live an immoral life rebel against God. Moab is the world today.

Pick of the Crop: Christ knows the beginning from the end. He understands your case and will justly mete out sentence. His laws are for our well-being. If we choose to live contrary to His commands, we invite His righteous judgment upon our lives. Fall under the tender mercies of the Judge of all the Earth in sweet obedience and live.

3 A Famine in the House of Bread

"...there was a famine in the land." Ruth 1:1

We find there was a famine in the land of the house of bread and praise (Bethlehem, Judah). That's an astonishing paradox. God's people have worked to bring the land of milk and honey to a place of brambles and briers. It's not our Lord who's wanting. He says, "If I were hungry, I would not tell you; for the world is Mine, and all its fullness" (Psalm 50:12). God is in need of nothing. He supplies rain for the fields and food for the fowl. Your next breath is a gift of His grace. The drought is in the heart of the people who fail to trust in God. His people repeatedly fall into idolatry by serving the gods around them.

How many of us have walked in like manner? We have been ruled by our passions and influenced by the world around us, following after lying vanities which pacify for a moment. The famine comes to correct us. "'Also I gave you cleanness of teeth in all your cities, and lack of bread in all your places; yet you have not returned to Me,' says the Lord" (Amos 4:6). Instead we go out from God to live in the country of Moab, where no joy or gladness is found.

> Joy and gladness are taken
> From the plentiful field
> And from the land of Moab;
> I have caused wine to fail from the winepresses;
> No one will tread with joyous shouting—
> Not joyous shouting! (Jeremiah 48:33)

God may send a drought to devour your resources or His east wind to dry your well (Hosea 13:15). The famine is a prelude of things to come.

A famine is on the horizon, and it's poised to cover the world as we know it like clouds in the sky. The church has been an oasis for those wandering in the wilderness of this world. It has been a storehouse for the famished, but it is showing signs of wasting.

There's a famine of hearing the Word of God in what represents the house of bread and praise. Many of the world's churches are preaching, teaching, and singing the methodologies of this world. The pulpit has become pliable. Pastors are fearful to "preach the word! Be ready in season and out of season. Convince, rebuke, exhort, with all longsuffering and teaching" (2 Timothy 4:2).

There is a famine in many churches today. Preachers refuse to read the Truth, hear the Truth, and teach the Truth. Pontius Pilate, Rome's procurator and governor of Judaea, had the epitome of truth standing before him and cynically asked, "What is truth?" There are many preachers today asking the same question. "Now the Spirit expressly says that in latter times some will depart from the faith, giving heed to deceiving spirits and doctrines of demons" (1 Timothy 4:1). These churches are lusting for preachers, teachers, prophets, and priests who willingly lie so that the people will forget the name of God (Jeremiah 23:25–27).

Their condition shows little signs of improvement. "For the time will come when they will not endure sound doctrine, but according to their own desires, because they have itching ears, they will heap up for themselves teachers; and they will turn their ears away from the truth, and be turned aside to fables" (2 Timothy 4:3–4).

There's a famine in the church, giving ground to seeds that thrive in a desert climate. Entertainment has entered the ecumenical environment, taking center stage, stimulating the senses while desensitizing the way of the Spirit. With the damage done, these weeds tumble through another group or congregation, disbursing spores along the way. Sins, lies, and lusts flourish in a famine, and to make matters worse, "My people love to have it so" (Jeremiah 5:31).

There's a famine in our land. "Justice is turned back, and righteousness stands afar off; for truth is fallen in the street, and equity cannot enter" (Isaiah 59:14). Agendas govern decisions. Instead of following God's laws, feelings are followed. "Woe to those who call evil good, and good evil; who put darkness for light, and light for darkness; who put bitter for sweet, and sweet for bitter" (Isaiah 5:20).

God sends a famine, hoping His people will return and follow Him. Instead, we flee to Moab. Are you experiencing dry, barren times in your walk? Has heaven's dew ceased? Is your zeal for God gone? Take heed. A famine may be upon you. "'Behold, the days are coming,' says the Lord God, 'that I will send a famine on the land, not a famine of bread, nor a thirst for water, but of hearing the words of the Lord.'" (Amos 8:11). Without hearing the Word of God, we're lost. Without His Word, we lack direction. Multitudes have attempted to plot a course in this world without God only to be found wandering through life's weary wilderness on the plains of self-destruction.

Pick of the Crop: If you love the Lamb of God, Christ Jesus, you'll feed His sheep. The church, God's people, have been given the Bread of Life that we might give to those who hunger. Should you, Christian, be found anemic as a result of famine, where shall other weary, hungry souls find nourishment? When Christ fed the multitudes, He blessed, broke, and gave the bread to His disciples so the disciples would give it to the people (Matthew 14:19). When time comes, will you have that spiritual bread to feed the famished? Will you?

4 Elimelech and His Family

"The name of the man was Elimelech, the name of his wife was Naomi, and the names of his two sons were Mahlon and Chilion—Ephrathites of Bethlehem, Judah. And they went to the country of Moab and remained there." Ruth 1:2

Elimelech placed a great burden upon his family fleeing Judah for Moab from the correction of God. The famine was not for the nation only, but also for the man himself. Famine is a calling card of God, calling the man to repentance.

His name was Elimelech, which means, "My God is king." The name signifies his relation to God as a godly man and a shepherd in his home, but was he? He was to lead by example, to guide and encourage his flock, that is, his family. Why and how did this man end up in Moab?

There are people carrying the Lord in name only. They're nominal, testifying of a calling from God, but the life they live is contrary to that call. Is there famine in your home? Is there a famine within your soul? Have you fled home or church in hopes of greener pastures? Are you shepherding your flock? Fleeing the famine in Bethlehem will only intensify the drought.

Poor decisions place your family in great danger. Elimelech's intent was to sojourn, to tarry temporarily, and when conditions improved, to return to Bethlehem. And God recorded his choices for all eternity. Believe it, men. Everything you do is recorded, whether good or bad. "For we must all appear before the judgment seat of Christ, that each one may receive the things done in the body, according to what he has done, whether good or bad" (2 Corinthians 5:10).

Elimelech was an Ephrathite a descendant of Ephraim the second son of Joseph (Genesis 46:20). The family name means "a double fruitfulness." Elimelech's wife was Naomi, which means "pleasant." A pleasant wife is a good thing for man, and Elimelech found God's favor in her. He had two sons, Mahlon, means "sickly" and Chilion, meaning "pining" or "failing in health." How could a fruitful (Ephrathite) family from the house of bread and praise become so diseased?

Pick of the Crop: A man's family is a gift from the hands of God. A virtuous wife is a crown gracing the head of her husband (Proverbs 12:4). "Behold, children are a heritage from the Lord, the fruit of the womb *is* a reward. Like arrows in the hand of a warrior, so are the children of one's youth" (Psalm 127:3–4). The world is attacking your beautiful family. It wants to destroy them. Husbands, labor to place your family in a position to succeed, overcoming the world, the flesh, and the devil. If you're living in Moab accepting the favors of this world, you've already set your family up for failure. Men, ask God to give you victory over the lures of this world for your sake as well as your family.

5 SIN

Elimelech's once fruitful family was sickly as a result of sin. "For all have sinned and fall short of the glory of God" (Romans 3:23). From the pious parliamentarian to the pitiful peasant, all have sinned. Sin has permeated into the very length of our loins to the center of the souls of mankind. No one has passed through this world unscathed.

The poor health of Elimelech's sons did not necessarily reflect a sinful life; rather, as a result of sin we're all doomed to die both spiritually and physically. But praise be to God, Christ has become our balm, a soothing salve to save the spiritually dead soul from sin.

When anyone takes Christ by faith and begins to apply the rich ointment of His love over a sin-sickened heart, His love immediately pulsates through our total being. His Spirit seeks out and covers our spiritual disease, until over time He completely eradicates it. He's working, healing, moment by moment, day by day. We must trust His work by faith. We ingest pills and elixirs for physical diseases by faith, trusting in a favorable result. How much more shall we trust Christ's healing work within our souls?

But you say, "I've tried Christ and keep re-infecting myself by living in this sinful world. What more shall I do?" The answer is always to return to Christ. "If we confess our sins, He is faithful and just to forgive us our sins and to cleanse us from all unrighteousness" (1 John 1:9). The healing power of Christ will never fail. "Therefore He is also able to save to the uttermost those who come to God through Him, since He always lives to make intercession for them" (Hebrews 7:25).

Is your soul saved and secured by faith in Christ but your body isn't showing signs of renewed vigor? It's not unrealistic to trust Jesus for healing with the same power demonstrated to the multitudes over and over again in His Word. The natural course of this world is disease and death. We cannot escape it. But He is the God of the natural and the supernatural for all who believe.

"Yet man is born to trouble, as the sparks fly upward" (Job 5:7). Troubled souls, weakened flesh—they are both a part of life. "Therefore we do not lose heart. Even though our outward man is perishing, yet the inward man is being renewed day by day" (2 Corinthians 4:16). You can have a healthy, vibrant, living soul dwelling in the midst of a decaying body, if you'll only heed the call of Christ by faith.

Elimelech never turned back to Bethlehem to the security of the Sovereign. "And they went to the country of Moab and remained there" (Ruth 1:2). Moab was a remote relative of Israel. Lot, Abraham's nephew (Genesis 12:5) had an incestuous relationship with his two daughters while drunk with wine, which was entirely a plot of his daughters. Two sons came of that encounter, Moab and Ammon. Both became founders of nations (Genesis 19:30–38).

Pick of the Crop: A vesicle is discovered on your flesh. Over time it grows and begins to seep a purulent discharge. It looks disturbing. You try to conceal it. Years go by with no improvement, and the lesion begins to emit a foul pungent odor. The wisdom of this world has no cure for it, and you eventually succumb to your ailment. This is like man's sin before God, and yet He has given a remedy, His righteous son. O taste and see.

6 Death in Moab

"Then Elimelech, Naomi's husband, died; and she was left, and her two sons. Now they took wives of the women of Moab: the name of the one was Orpah, and the name of the other Ruth. And they dwelt there about ten years." Ruth 1:3–4

If you're living for the world, you'll die in the world. "Strike the Shepherd, and the sheep will be scattered" (Mark 14:27). At the apprehension of Christ, His sheep-like disciples scattered in fear of their lives, bringing the ministry to a halt. Some even returned to their former professions as if the lessons of our Lord were never learned. Elimelech, the shepherd of his home, died, leaving his family in a vulnerable position.

"Now they took wives of the women of Moab" (Ruth 1:4). After the death of Elimelech, the two sons married women of Moab. Mahlon and Chilion became unequally joined, that is, married to unbelievers. "Do not be unequally yoked together with unbelievers. For what fellowship has righteousness with lawlessness? And what communion has light with darkness?" (2 Corinthians 6:14). They married women who did not serve the God of the Hebrews. These women served other gods. Their ways and traditions were strange. The onset of their marriage bond, that is to say, their yoke of matrimony, was uneven. These couples cannot labor together in the things of God. This is the danger facing young and old in this world today. Without the guidance of the Shepherd, an indelible, unequal yoke of marriage awaits.

Picture for a moment two beasts of burden, preparing to plow the field, secured together around their necks with a yoke. When one moves forward, so does the other. When one moves back or stops, so will the other. The two have learned to labor in-sync. The two are equally yoked.

Now imagine an ox and a mule joined by a yoke. From the onset the two are unequal and both are stubborn. When one moves forward, the other kicks, pulling back in an attempt to separate; until finally it collapses refusing to budge. This concept is forbidden in the law. How much more so the joining of two souls? "You shall not plow with an ox and a donkey together" (Deuteronomy 22:10).

The yoke, among other things, speaks of submission, service, and strength. A yoke is for our good, our control, and our employment. Don't greet the yoke under the guise of something grievous. Christ said, "My yoke is easy and My burden is light" (Matthew 11:30). Why plow alone? Be yoked with Christ. When two are equally yoked, submission has twice the strength—two times the service—which equals a greater increase of our labors.

Most marriages begin the wrong way. Marriage vows have become vacuous. Solemn ceremonies are diminished to a song and a dance. God's authoritative marriage manual, the Bible, is viewed as an obstacle in the eyes of the world today. Elimelech's sons' marriages were in jeopardy from the start.

How quick we are to forget past weights and sins that have caused us to stumble. Balak, ruler of Moab, attempted multiple times to curse the people of God (Numbers 22–24). Israel committed whoredom with the daughters of Moab, ate at their sacrifices, bowed down to their gods, and joined in their worship service at Baal-peor (Numbers 25:3).

Husbands, the decisions you make will be felt by your family long after death. Your decision has the ability to bless or curse. Take time to review the history of the man named Lot, who chose to live within the surroundings of the city of Sodom, placing his family in great danger (Genesis 19). The Lord called, but Lot lingered in his lust. Yet, the mercies of God saved him from the judgment that fell on that perverse city, but not so with his wife who disobeyed the commandment of the

Lord. And in the weeks that followed, Lot reaped further consequences of living in the city of sin through the actions of his daughters.

Pick of the Crop: Living according to the ways of this world means death. With an affinity for this world's culture, our family decisions, marriages, religions, and daily choices will be worth nothing, but there is hope. "For if you live according to the flesh you will die, but if by the Spirit you put to death the deeds of the body, you will live" (Romans 8:13). Ask God to give you a greater love for Him and to separate you from the death that is in this world.

7 A Cry Out to Men

There's a rise in single parent homes. Most are managed by mothers or grandmothers who will love a child, as most mothers and grandmothers do. But where are the men?! More homes are missing fathers to lead, counsel, provide, protect, comfort, and love as most fathers do.

Harken to the harbingers: where are the fathers for the young sons to follow? Fathers have failed to finish their vocation. Men, you may be walking on the top side of this earth, but in God's eyes you're as dead as Elimelech. You've failed to instruct your son's while they were boys and omitted the pitfalls of growth and development as young adults. Your absenteeism increases the propensity of your sons neglecting their families. Sons need fathers to fashion their lives after. In your non-attendance, you've relinquished your God-given right to aid in the molding of sons to men. You've left the door wide open to a sinful world, and the passions of this world will assuredly shape the tender hearts of your children into the image of godlessness!

Men, do your children see you standing beside their mother striving to obey the voice of God? Does your family see you serving God's people in some way? Are you even saved? Don't abandon your families! Most fathers today are blazing a trail to Moab with satchels full of excuses. God has put a call out, calling men back to Himself and back to their families, but most are dull of hearing. Pray to God to pierce their souls, "'to turn the hearts of the fathers to the children,' and the disobedient to the wisdom of the just, to make ready a people prepared for the Lord" (Luke 1:17).

Korah, Dathan, and Abiram—three men decided to rebel against God and Moses pertaining to the priesthood (that is, religious activities), and they died in their rebellion (Numbers 16).

Read the account of a man named Achan, who loved the riches of this world rather than the richness that comes in obeying the Word of God. He perished along with the things he lusted after (Joshua 7).

These were family men who lost their families as the result of poor decisions. Life and death are demonstrated in the decisions made for God or for ourselves. As long as he had breath, Elimelech had opportunity to return home with his family and did not. Don't abandon your family to Moab. Reconcile them back to Bethlehem, back to the love of God.

Failing fathers and missing men are becoming carnage littering the spiritual battlefields of this world. Men have been wounded and left to die, severed by the subtle and sometimes blatant arsenal of the culture, weapons designed to remove the fathers from their families. Men with little to no motivation are making poor decisions. They are quick to respond to the pleasures of the moment, rather than the peace that comes with patience, living a temperate life before Christ.

Pick of the Crop: Men have failed to follow the Word of God for guidance while attempting to maneuver their families through life's battlefields. Ask God to awaken the hearts of the fathers in this world to return to Christ and their family. If you're one who has been wounded in the war against your soul, call out to God now. He's waiting to save you.

8 ORPAH AND RUTH

"The name of the one was Orpah, and the name of the other Ruth." Ruth 1:4

Orpah means "mane, back of the neck, stiff neck." This trait is found in all mankind, some in greater degree than others. Wives, are you stubborn in your ways? Do you excuse yourself, saying, "This is me. This is who I am"? If that's true, God has a work to do within you. "Better to dwell in the wilderness, than with a contentious and angry woman" (Proverbs 21:19).

Women, true godly men are in short supply placing you in a quagmire. Don't drive your man away by a stiff-necked, stubborn spirit. Without the power of God, your man won't have the backbone to endure. Contrast the name Orpah with the name Ruth. Ruth means "friend." It's a lovely union to observe marriages between friends.

Both of these women are identified as being of Moab, and the revelation of their true character remains to be seen. God's furnace of affliction has a way of revealing the true person when the dross is removed.

Two ill Hebrew men married strangers—two Gentile women, who helped the men in their afflicted state, which was comforting to the heart of Naomi. We read in Luke 10:25–37 where another Hebrew lay with hands stretched toward the threshold of death until a stranger—a Gentile—found him, befriended him, had compassion on him, and mended his wounds. The stranger loved him, not in vain babbling, but in demonstrable deeds.

All have the disease of father Adam passed down through generations. It leaves men and women sickly frail, fragile of flesh and soul, so let us come to Jesus. Be united to Him in marriage. He's a friend to the sick in heart. "Those who are well have no need of a physician, but those who are sick" (Matthew 9:12).

There came a time in Israel's history when she became estranged and grew apart from God's affectionate love. "They are all estranged from Me by their idols" (Ezekiel 14:5). In doing so the health of the people became infirmed.

> "Why should you be stricken again?
> You will revolt more and more.
> The whole head is sick,
> And the whole heart faints.
> From the sole of the foot even to the head,
> There is no soundness in it,
> But wounds and bruises and putrefying sores;
> They have not been closed or bound up,
> Or soothed with ointment.
> Your country is desolate,
> Your cities are burned with fire;
> Strangers devour your land in your presence;
> And it is desolate, as overthrown by strangers"
> (Isaiah 1:5–7).

But God, in His great love toward His people, would send aid to His ailing flock during diverse times, in some instances from the hands of Gentiles.

We have here a marriage between two nations. One nation is of this world; the other nation, when following God, is heavenly centered. One nation serves the gods of this world; the other nation worships the Lord of Glory.

The two men are diseased in their body with a knowledge of God. The two women are ailing souls without a knowledge of God. With whom or what have you become yoked in marriage? Is your marriage nothing more in your eyes than a joining together of two bodies? Can your marriage bring healing power to your soul? God puts greater value on your inner life than that flesh you're dwelling in. Marriages are to bring the individuals to an exalted way of living in the eyes of the world around, offering an example to follow. "Marriage is honorable among all, and the bed undefiled; but fornicators and adulterers God will judge" (Hebrews 13:4).

Pick of the Crop: A union will occur between Jews and Gentiles. The providence of God will create one out of two. Israel is ailing and the Gentiles are lost, but in the fullness of time God will heal His people and complete the work of salvation in the Gentile. "There is neither Greek nor Jew, circumcised nor uncircumcised, barbarian, Scythian, slave nor free, but Christ is all and in all" (Colossians 3:11). Israel and the Church will be one. Ask God to give you a heart and eyes to understand and see His worldwide plan for the nations.

9 Ten Year Tribulation

"They dwelt there about ten years. Then both Mahlon and Chilion also died; so the woman survived her two sons and her husband." Ruth 1:4b–5

Notice the progression in Ruth 1:1–4. They "went to dwell" (v1) and "remained" (v2). "Naomi's husband died" (v3). Her sons married "women of Moab" and "dwelt there about ten years" (v4). Many stories are told of sojourners turning aside in the way only to become permanent residents in the graves of strange lands. "O Israel, thou hast destroyed thyself; but in me is thine help" (Hosea 13:9 KJV). Ten years of trials and testing, ending in death. Pray to God your life does not end this way in Moab.

Here again the decisions we make are far felt for life or death, blessings or cursings. This family has traveled great distances to separate themselves from famine, and we discover a more severe famine raging within the family of Elimelech. There's no life worth living outside of God. The men of Bethlehem who went to dwell in Moab would have agreed. They had ten years of testing, stricken strength, serving in Moab. Moab is the barren wilderness of this world. Your time, energy, health, and wealth are quickly consumed in Moab. Moab will devour your family, your children's future, your life, and ultimately your soul.

In years past, Egypt, as with Moab, stood symbolic of this world's culture. Living in Egypt was living in the world away from God's Promised Land. Pain and suffering accompanies the child of God who fashions their life after the customs and culture of this world. "So the Egyptians made the children of Israel serve with rigor. And they made their lives bitter with hard bondage—in mortar, in brick, and in all manner of service in the field. All their service in which they made them serve was with rigor" (Exodus 1:13–14).

The world is a cruel taskmaster toward the people of God. The focus of this world's principalities and powers is death to those who stand for righteousness. We who are called to live for Christ are in a spiritual battle for our souls. "For we do not wrestle against flesh and blood, but against principalities, against powers, against the rulers of the darkness of this age, against spiritual hosts of wickedness in the heavenly places" (Ephesians 6:12).

In Egypt, the culture of the world sought to kill all the sons of the seed of Israel in an attempt to whittle away their strength. Further still, a satanic scheme in the spiritual world was unfolding—a plot to strike a blow against the seed of the coming Messiah. "And he said, 'When you do the duties of a midwife for the Hebrew women, and see them on the birthstools, if it is a son, then you shall kill him; but if it is a daughter, then she shall live.' But the midwives feared God, and did not do as the king of Egypt commanded them, but saved the male children alive" (Exodus 1:16–17). The world and the devil hate the seed of God and daily seek opportunity for our demise.

They lived ten long years in Moab under cruel conditions. Finally, all the men of Bethlehem who made the journey with Naomi died, along with the potential Messianic seed. The death of the men was a victory for the rulers of darkness. Men in the service of God have a responsibility to refrain from the fantasies of this world. Within their loins are potential preachers and teachers of righteousness, light to a dark world, salt where there is no savor. Men, return to God! Flee Moab and live!

Are there similarities between their lives and ours? Was the journey home to Bethlehem impossible for the waning, wearied, and weak? Had following the commandments of God become too burdensome? When Christians wander away from God, their divine service to Him becomes difficult at best. An eagle could no more fly with wings clipped than a fish could swim without fins. The same is true in the life of the people of God. When we remove ourselves from obeying His Word, we are doomed to fail. The hopes of soaring to heavenly heights are stunted, and the desire to probe the depths of God's ocean of untold treasures ends in utter disappointment.

Pick of the Crop: Living apart from the people of God—without fellowship or hearing the Word of God—will bring about a wasted, unhealthy spiritual life. Your ability to love others as God has loved you will be stymied. Break this spiritual cycle while you have breath and be healed. Cry out to God and live.

10 Return to Judah

> **"Then she arose with her daughters-in-law that she might return from the country of Moab, for she had heard in the country of Moab that the Lord had visited His people by giving them bread. Therefore she went out from the place where she was, and her two daughters-in-law with her; and they went on the way to return to the land of Judah." Ruth 1:6–7**

Sins against God leave a nation and its people in jeopardy. Woe to the nation who swears as a mighty chorus against the ways of God, a nation that is enamored with adultery and murder. Leaders lie, statesmen steal, and multiple gods are glorified in supreme grandeur. God will judge!

Moab and similar adversaries are waiting in the wings to be used by God to bring judgment upon His people. When Israel continued to sin before the face of God, God strengthened Eglon, king of Moab. He, along with the nation of Ammon and Amalek, crossed the Jordan River into the Promised Land and afflicted Israel by capturing the City of Palm Trees, which is Jericho.

If we let it, sin will enter into the promises God has for you and your family, consuming God's blessings over your life. The appetite of Moab is morbid, characterized by their portly king. So too is the appetite of sin. Eighteen years did Israel serve the king of Moab, but when Israel cried out to God, He sent a deliverer, a savior by the name of Ehud ("to unite"). In the midst of a sinful nation, Ehud responded to the call of God on his life, desiring to unite the people and nation back to God and deliver them from the burden of Moab.

How long have you been serving sin in your life? Can you see God's best for you being devoured by your adversary as did Naomi? Call out to God. "The Lord your God in your midst, The Mighty One, will save; He will rejoice over you with gladness, He will quiet you with His love, He will rejoice over you with singing" (Zephaniah 3:17).

Ehud made a two-edge sword and went to the king of Moab with the Word of God. When the two men were alone in the king's summer parlor, Ehud took out his sword and thrust it into the king's abdomen, killing him. Ehud escaped, and that day Moab was defeated by Israel (Judges 3:12–30).

How does this apply to my life, you ask? No matter how long you've been enslaved to sin nor how large a mess you are mired in, victory is waiting through "the sword of the Spirit, which is the word of God" (Ephesians 6:17). Naomi saw what Moab had stolen from her and her family. Now she would trust the Word of God for a victory she could not see.

Pick of the Crop: Our many enemies seek to oppress and suppress, but there is a God in heaven who sees. When we return to God, in that decision we're literally returning to praise Him. A joyful celebration will greet you in due season, and the enemy who muzzled your mouth will be found no more. Sing a joyful song unto God and praise His holy name!

11 THE CALL

"Then she arose with her daughters-in-law" Ruth 1:6

The death of Naomi's desires became her awakening. Then she arose. There's one direction for the lowly, and that's up. Naomi had suffered tremendously, three blows to body, soul, and spirit. The men that were to her as arrows—her strength, her future in seed for generations to come—were all dead. No words from these men were recorded; nevertheless, their actions sound through eternity.

To this junction in the journey of souls Jehovah-Jireh

("The Lord will provide") brings us. During the hardest times of our lives comes the softening of the heart, the breaking of the will, and the dying of self. At our lowest state in Him, we begin to arise. The call is open to all. There's a call to the sinner as well as the saint who may have lost their way, climaxing to that final call: "And the Spirit and the bride say, 'Come!' And let him who hears say, 'Come!' And let him who thirsts come. Whoever desires, let him take the water of life freely" (Revelation 22:17).

Notice, Naomi's journey was not alone, but others who have been afflicted with like sufferings were drawn. "She arose with her daughters-in-law." O the lovely mercies of God! He has not left us alone. He stepped out of eternity for us, "for the Son of Man has come to seek and to save that which was lost" (Luke 19:10).

"She had heard in the country of Moab that the Lord had visited His people by giving them bread" (Ruth 1:6). The soul of Naomi responded to those gracious words. The giver of bread is Jesus.

Jesus is the Bread of Life. "I am the bread of life. He who comes to Me shall never hunger, and he who believes in Me shall never thirst" (John 6:35).

Jesus is the bread that came down from heaven (John 6:41).

Jesus is that Living Bread from heaven. "If anyone eats of this bread, he will live forever; and the bread that I shall give is My flesh, which I shall give for the life of the world" (John 6:51).

"Oh, taste and see that the Lord is good. Blessed is the man who trusts in Him" (Psalm 34:8). The eating of Christ, the Living Bread, is feeding our hungry souls on His Word, the Holy Scriptures. Reading, praying, meditating on Him all are ways of nourishing the soul. O that the hungry would wait patiently for His daily bread and not flee to Moab for nourishment!

Read the account of King Nebuchadnezzar at the time when he heard the call of God on his life. He was thrust from men to abide with the beasts. Yet, he returns to his throne through the call of God. "I, Nebuchadnezzar, lifted my eyes to heaven, and my understanding returned to me; and I blessed the Most High and praised and honored Him who lives forever: For His dominion is an everlasting dominion, and His kingdom is from generation to generation" (Daniel 4:34).

A spiritually dead son, lost in a faraway land, separated from the tender love of his father, when he heard the call of God, "he came to himself" and returned home (Luke 15:11–32). The disciple Peter had left the ministry and returned to his fishing profession. When he heard the call of God, he cast himself into the sea and swam to shore, eager to be with his Savior who called. (John 21).

The call of God is His way of moving His own out of one area of life into another. Nebuchadnezzar heard the call of God living in the wild. A wayward son heard the call of God dining among swine. A distraught disciple heard the call of God while adrift on the sea. Naomi heard the call of God in Moab.

What place have you come to in your journey? Have you heard the sweet whisper calling you out, calling you back to Bethlehem, back to

God? Don't hesitate to heed His call—a sweet, gentle touch of soul. Arise and return to God. Arise now.

Pick of the Crop: All will hear the call of God, a personal call in a language understood by your soul. Today, if you hear His voice, "harden not your hearts, as in the provocation" (Hebrews 3:8 KJV). Whether you hear or forbear, the choice is yours alone.

12 The Way of Holiness

"And they went on the way to return to the land of Judah." Ruth 1:7

Again we see Orpah and Ruth walking with Naomi in the way of holiness. "And an highway shall be there, and a way, and it shall be called the way of holiness; the unclean shall not pass over it; but it shall be for those: the wayfaring men, though fools, shall not err therein" (Isaiah 35:8 KJV). This way is living a holy life, a new path to travel in this sinful world. This path will lead you through this world, out of the land of Moab, into that Holy City, God's promise with streets of gold in glory (Revelation 21:21). Keep this in mind: when you're walking the way of holiness, your back is always toward Moab.

The women are heading to the land of Judah, the land of praise, the Promised Land of God. There was joy in heaven over their decision to turn away from Moab and return to Bethlehem. "There will be more joy in heaven over one sinner who repents than over ninety-nine just persons who need no repentance" (Luke 15:7). Be not dismayed, lover of God. Heaven is keenly aware of our earthly struggles, and its occupants are cheering us along the way.

In Moab, there were three widows. There was devastation, disease, and death. No fruit of the womb. Why would we stay there? O that we would return to the land of praise. It is waiting "to console those who mourn in Zion, to give them beauty for ashes, the oil of joy for mourning, the garment of praise for the spirit of heaviness; that they may be called trees of righteousness, the planting of the Lord, that He may be glorified" (Isaiah 61:3). Sinner, come out of Moab while there's time and flee to

Bethlehem! There you'll find joy and celebration. Christian friend, if you're in Moab without the leading of God, come out! Return to Bethlehem where there's gladness of heart.

Pick of the Crop: The way of holiness is a narrow path bearing the beautiful feet of the lover of God. The directions are found in the Holy Scriptures. The road may be rough at times, but be encouraged our Lord has gone before us. Shout for joy and be glad you have found the way!

13 Speaking the Language of Moab

"And Naomi said to her two daughters–in-law, 'Go, return each to her mother's house. The Lord deal kindly with you, as you have dealt with the dead and with me. The Lord grant that you may find rest, each in the house of her husband.' So she kissed them, and they lifted up their voices and wept." Ruth 1:8–9

In Moab, Naomi learned to communicate with the Moabites, enhancing her assimilation. Living in the culture of the world, away from God, you too will learn to communicate with the language of the world, enhancing your indoctrination into the current age.

"Go, return each to her mother's house."

Naomi encouraged her daughters-in-law to return to their mothers' homes. She spoke well of Orpah and Ruth, trusting the Lord would deal kindly because they had been kind to her sons. The death of her sons was the final blow for Naomi.

". . . find rest, each in the house of her husband."

The daughters-in-law were kind to Elimelech's family, and Naomi expressed pleasant words in the hopes that the Lord would grant them rest in the homes of new husbands. She offered each an affectionate kiss, and they all wept.

The language of Moab is to eat, drink, and be merry. It is an immediate gratification of the flesh and its desires. The language of Moab has no true word for life after this world. The hope of heaven's higher ground and the call to holy living are not spoken. The language of Moab reverberates in the present moment. Naomi spoke directly to the heart of these two young women while they wept.

Finally we're given a glimpse into the hearts of these women. They were crying over years of grief; in their horizons loomed a languishing and loneliness of soul. But must it come? Christ came from heaven that we might go to heaven; He died that we might live. Where there was no way, He made a way. Be assured, the tears Naomi shed on the drab plane of Moab were recovered and recorded by God. "You number my wanderings; put my tears into Your bottle. Are they not in Your book?" (Psalm 56:8). Naomi's day of reckoning would come.

Pick of the Crop: Speaking the language of Moab—the world—keeps the hungry soul away from the house of bread. The vernacular is understood by those living according to the ways of the world, but the lover of God hears a different voice among the sounding brass and tinkling cymbal of the culture. Ask the Lord to give you an ear to hear His sweet voice and not the sounds of another.

14 We Will Return with You

"And they said to her, 'Surely we will return with you to your people.'" Ruth 1:10

After years of silence, now we hear from the women of Moab. They wanted to return to Bethlehem with Naomi. For a disciple at this step on the road, the cost of discipleship must be weighed. The Christian life is a beautiful life, but there're many challenges along the way. Naomi was aware of the challenges and began to prepare her daughters-in-law.

Challenges that arise in the life of the Christian can be boiled down to obeying or disobeying God. The standards of the world are not the standards of those who are called of God. The world celebrates sexual sins, but for the lover of God, "this is the will of God, your sanctification: that you should abstain from sexual immorality" (1 Thessalonians 4:3). The world molds and fashions multiple gods. God declares, "You shall have no other gods before Me" (Exodus 20:3). This world reports to have many ways to God. Jesus said, "I am the way, the truth, and the life. No one comes to the Father except through Me" (John 14:6). Those Scriptures along with many more reveal differences between the people of God and those who strive after the ways, traditions, and values of this age.

The two Moabite women were eager to continue the trip on a road they had never traveled, but there was hesitancy within Naomi, a precautionary pause. She knew the opposition her companions may face.

"...If anyone desires to come after Me, let him deny himself, and take up his cross daily, and follow Me" (Luke 9:23). If you truly desire to leave Moab for the Promised Land, there's a cross you must bear. With the cross there is a cost. Although our debt has been paid, we as His disciples must give up our will for His. We are to follow in His steps. The Christ King gave up His will to His Father. We—you and me—must be willing to first deny ourselves. Self-denial is learning to live a temperate life, a life of restraint where sobriety within our lives radiates like a sweet-smelling ointment. We learn to say no to whatever is not pleasing to God.

Next, you must take up your cross daily to follow Christ.

We learn to think as He thinks: "Let this mind be in you which was also in Christ Jesus" (Philippians 2:5).

Speak as He speaks: "If anyone speaks, let him speak as the oracles of God" (1 Peter 4:11).

Live as He lives in this world: "A new commandment I give to you, that you love one another; as I have loved you, that you also love one another. By this all will know that you are My disciples, if you have love for one another" (John 13:34–35).

The cross speaks of suffering, shame, pain, and ultimately death, death to ourselves and the things of this world. Our death is short-lived. On the other side of the cross, there's life eternal and fullness of joy. "For the joy that was set before Him endured the cross, despising the shame, and has sat down at the right hand of the throne of God" (Hebrews 12:2).

Bearing your cross keeps you in the mindset of dying. All are destined to die, the question is, will you die for the things of this world or die for Christ?

Bearing your cross may consist of being ridiculed by family and former friends while taking a stand for Christ. Faithfully bear your cross. You or a loved one may have a physical or emotional ailment that seems too difficult to bear. Bear your cross. Marriage unmanageable? Bear your cross. And if you die a martyr's death for Christ, faithfully bear your cross. There are many crosses, many lives. There's a cross perfectly fitted for you and for me.

Pick of the Crop: The eager in spirit may want to walk the road of discipleship but "have no root in themselves, and so endure only for a time. Afterward, when tribulation or persecution arises for the word's sake, immediately they stumble" (Mark 4:17). Bearing your cross causes offences, and the desire to travel the road to peace with God is overshadowed by those who oppose the cross. Should your decision waiver, you'll find yourself turning back to Moab. Ask the Lord to keep you in all your ways in whatsoever your cross may bring.

15 Please, Turn Back

"But Naomi said, 'Turn back, my daughters; why will you go with me? Are there still sons in my womb, that they may be your husbands? Turn back, my daughters, go—for I am too old to have a husband. If I should say I have hope, if I should have a husband tonight and should also bear sons, would you wait for them till they were grown? Would you restrain yourselves from having husbands? No, my daughters; for it grieves me very much for your sakes that the hand of the Lord has gone out against me!'" Ruth 1:11–13

Naomi asked, "Why will you go with me, for potential husbands? Why make the commitment to Bethlehem Ephrathah? It's an extremely small city among the people of Judah (Micah 5:2). Are you traveling for hidden desires and deceitful delight, or could there be a loftier, more heavenly passion?"

Many in the days of our Lord sought His company solely for selfish reasons, "Most assuredly, I say to you, you seek Me, not because you saw the signs, but because you ate of the loaves and were filled" (John 6:26). Many flocked to Christ to fill their bellies. The flesh is like the leech's daughters crying, "Give, give!" (Proverbs 30:15). Ever consuming is the flesh's visceral passions. Naomi instructed the two to move on with their lives. The heavenly call is a call for life, a soul must completely be submitted to its journey.

". . . for I am too old to have a husband. If I should say I have hope . . ."

She counseled them with reason. "If I should say I have hope," hope of finding a husband, hope of conception, hope of bearing sons. No, impossible. However, "the things which are impossible with men are possible with God" (Luke 18:27). The Bible speaks fondly of the patriarch Abraham, "who, contrary to hope, in hope believed, so that he became the father of many nations, according to what was spoken, 'so shall your descendants be'" (Romans 4:18). Naomi's age testified against her as did Abraham and Sarah, his wife.

Time is a humbling tool of God, who inhabits eternity (Isaiah 57:15). He spoke to Abraham when he was seventy-five years old, promising to make him a great nation (Genesis 12:2, 4). Twenty-four years later at ninety-nine years old, Abraham heard the promise reaffirmed (Genesis 17:1–5). Abraham laughed at the possibility of having a son in his old age, along with his wife, who was ninety years old (Genesis 17:17). But the promise of God stood true. When Abraham was one hundred, Sarah bore him a son and called his name Isaac, which means laughter (Genesis 21:1–5).

The hope Naomi had was failing. Her outward circumstances were daunting. All she could muster within her was the decision to obey the call to begin the journey home, back to Bethlehem.

Pick of the Crop: Ask yourself, "Why am I making the journey?" Is it for temporal pleasures? Don't go. Is it for signs and wonders? Journey no further. Are you traveling to please others? If so, remain in Moab. If you're not willing to suffer for the name of Christ, please turn back.

16 Losing Someone

"It grieves me very much for your sakes that the hand of the Lord has gone out against me!" Ruth 1:13

The death of the ones we love can be overwhelming. Naomi had grieved much for her daughters-in-law's losses as well as her own. Being out of fellowship with God creates such losses.

Consider Adam and Eve. After their sin, they lost the fellowship they had enjoyed with God. They attempted to conceal themselves by covering their shame with leaves, just as men do today with religion, a feeble attempt to repair one's relationship with God. "Then the eyes of both of them were opened, and they knew that they were naked; and they sewed fig leaves together and made themselves coverings" (Genesis 3:7).

Divine fellowship between God and mankind was lost, but the Lord God called and came seeking to redeem the man and his wife. "And they heard the sound of the Lord God walking in the garden in the cool of the day, and Adam and his wife hid themselves from the presence of the Lord God among the trees of the garden" (Genesis 3:8).

The couple lost fellowship with each other after they rebelled against God—the blame game (Genesis 3:12). They lost fellowship with the earth too. What was to be a pleasant place to live became a curse (Genesis 3:17–19). But God is not to be outdone. "For the earnest expectation of the creation eagerly waits for the revealing of the sons of God" (Romans 8:19).

God offers His plan for the covering of sin: redemption through the shedding of blood acceptable in His sight. "Also for Adam and his wife the Lord God made tunics of skin, and clothed them" (Genesis 3:21). In our mortality, life and death walk hand in hand closer than we can imagine. Something has to die in order to cover our transgressions—death for life.

These are allegories of things to come. "For whatever things were written before were written for our learning, that we through the patience and comfort of the Scriptures might have hope" (Romans 15:4). Adam and Eve's acceptance of God's covering placed them on the road to fellowship with God. We all must approach God on His terms. Naomi knew she had to heed the call and return to God and His way of life for her. Only God can make up for losses. The things we count as losses, those things which cause grief of soul in this earthly realm, are for our gain in glory. "So I will restore to you the years that the swarming locust has eaten . . . You shall eat in plenty and be satisfied, and praise the name of the Lord your God, who has dealt wondrously with you; and My people shall never be put to shame. Then you shall know that I am in the midst of Israel: I am the Lord your God, and there is no other. My people shall never be put to shame" (Joel 2:25–27).

Pick of the Crop: Have you suffered through the death and dying of a loved one? Do you recall the emotional journey you found yourself on? If it carried you to a greater understanding of your mortality, amen. God was also grieved at the loss of Adam and Eve, for in them all humanity died. We were lost spiritually, separated from God. "For as in Adam all die, even so in Christ all shall be made alive" (1 Corinthians 15:22).

17 RUTH WOULD NOT LEAVE

"Then they lifted up their voices and wept again; and Orpah kissed her mother-in-law, but Ruth clung to her. And she said, 'Look, your sister-in-law has gone back to her people and to her gods; return after your sister-in-law.'" Ruth 1:14–15

In the height of King David's difficulties, Ittai the Gittite, whose name means "near," desired nothing more than to be with his friend in death or life (2 Samuel 15:19–21). The same was said of Ruth. Consider this: Ruth cleaved to her mother-in-law. She drew close and would not let go. The Spirit of God within Naomi was wooing the soul of Ruth. We're now witnessing Ruth's attraction to God and His people. Ruth joined herself with Naomi in following God. Ruth accepted God's call and committed to Bethlehem.

Ruth held another spirit than that of her sister-in-law. Ruth held the Spirit of God Himself. She resolved to set her face like flint toward Judah. She counted the cost of the flesh, which paled compared to the eternal riches of a soul. "What profit is it to a man if he gains the whole world, and loses his own soul? Or what will a man give in exchange for his soul?" (Matthew 16:26). Nothing. All the wealth and good deeds contained in this world can never pay the price of one soul. An eternal soul needs an eternal recompense.

The Son of God, Christ Jesus, paid the price for our souls. It cost Him His sinless, spotless, precious life. That was the only price God would accept. No deed done in the flesh will atone for our sins against God. All must come to Jesus, the eternal God, for eternal salvation.

The cleaving of Ruth to Naomi is matched by the knitting of Jonathan's soul (King Saul's son) to David's. "…the soul of Jonathan was knit to the soul of David, and Jonathan loved him as his own soul" (1 Samuel 18:1). Ruth had a love for a God she did not know. Jonathan had a love for a king he'd come to know. David was anointed king of Israel (1 Samuel 16:1, 13).

Both Ruth and Jonathan abandoned their identities for the love of God and king. Ruth left her life and her desires to be with the ones her soul admired. She abandoned all and was found in awe. Jonathan abandoned his desire to be king to serve the one who would become king. He abandoned his robe, his garment, his sword, his bow, and his girdle. Jonathan cast all upon the anointed king of Israel. Ruth loved Naomi, and Jonathan loved David. Dear friends, pray God will hasten our willingness to abandon everything when He calls—yes, everything for the love of God and humanity.

Pick of the Crop: Ruth refused to leave her mother-in-law. Abandoning Naomi was as turning her back on God and her love for the people of God. There is a God-given attraction the followers of Christ possess toward one another, and then there is a special bond-witness of two that is heavenly, sealed, secured, beyond measure where only our spirits can bear witness. Naomi and Ruth had such a bond, so too David and Jonathan, and you will also if you continue in the journey.

18 Turning Back

"Look, your sister-in-law has gone back to her people and to her gods." Ruth 1:15

There are those who begin the journey to Bethlehem only to realize the cost is far too great on the flesh. They are not willing to release the life of reveling and sensual pleasures. The soul of Ruth desired to leave Moab. Reflecting on the possibility of no husband and learning that the hand of God was against her mother-in-law, Orpah kissed Naomi and swiftly returned to her people and her gods. These are the ones who "have no root in themselves, and so endure only for a time. Afterward, when tribulation or persecution arises for the word's sake, immediately they stumble" (Mark 4:17).

Did Orpah count the cost, considering what it would mean to walk the Bethlehem way on the road to life with God? Or were her eyes blinded by her adversary, the devil? Both are possible.

There are many in this world who are at crossroads in their life. Should I go to Bethlehem or remain in Moab, follow God or remain living for the world? The journey leading to Bethlehem is narrow and difficult at times. The way to Moab is broad, and many are on that road to destruction. "Enter by the narrow gate; for wide is the gate and broad is the way that leads to destruction, and there are many who go in by it. Because narrow is the gate and difficult is the way which leads to life, and there are few who find it" (Matthew 7:13–14).

The Apostle Paul gave warning to those in Rome that they would be cut off like a branch if they did not continue in God's goodness (Romans 11:19–22). He told the Colossian believers they would be presented in

His sight holy, unblameable, and unreproveable, if they continued in the faith with God, grounded and settled (Colossians 1:21–23).

Paul himself feared being rejected by God if he failed to live a life of temperance in the ways of Christ. "But I discipline my body and bring it into subjection, lest, when I have preached to others, I myself should become disqualified" (1 Corinthians 9:27).

Gustave Dore's "Naomi and Her Daughters In Law"

Orpah began the journey. She was on the road, looking toward Bethlehem, but did not continue. Orpah's affections moved toward Moab. Note closely, Orpah turns her back on God while on the road to Bethlehem.

The road to Moab is a road of familiarities, a path lined with old ways and habits that have matured for years. These ways are contrary to God. You'll discover less resistance on the Moab mile. Signs are duplicitous, promising fun and easy travel.

"Remember Lot's wife," Jesus warned us (Luke 17:32). Lot's family was instructed not to look back while on the road to salvation. "So it came to pass, when they had brought them outside, that he said, 'Escape for your life! Do not look behind you nor stay anywhere in the plain. Escape to the mountains, lest you be destroyed'" (Genesis 19:17). Looking back constitutes a desire for the life left behind, a longing for the perverse pleasures of this world.

Ruth's sister-in-law went back, because she first looked back in the imagination of her heart. Lot's wife also went back in the imagination of her heart. She glanced back at the satisfaction she received in Sodom and the fantasies fulfilled by the friends in Gomorrah. Her love for this world was greater than her love of God and family. Her settlement seared in the plains of Jordan. She was consumed by her passions and was made a pillar of salt, a testimony to all who accept deliverance and later reject it. "But his wife looked back behind him, and she became a pillar of salt" (Genesis 19:26). Don't turn your back on Christ, He has carried you too far. "How shall we escape if we neglect so great a salvation, which at the first began to be spoken by the Lord, and was confirmed to us by those who heard Him?" (Hebrews 2:3).

Pick of the Crop: Returning to what you have been delivered from is like a dog returning to its vomit (Proverbs 26:11). You're a fool to do so. Turning back is different from falling back. There are those who fall back into sin only to repent and return to a right standing with God, but the ones who turn back, refuse to heed the spirit of repentance and return to the repulsive sins from which they were delivered. Ask God to keep you on the narrow path of salvation and give you a desire not to look back into the world from whence you came.

19 Leave Your Baggage Behind

But Ruth said: "Entreat me not to leave you, or to turn back from following after you; for wherever you go, I will go; and wherever you lodge, I will lodge; your people shall be my people, and your God, my God. Where you die, I will die, and there will I be buried. The Lord do so to me, and more also, if anything but death parts you and me." Ruth 1:16–17

Ruth knew turning back to Moab wasn't an option for her. Going back to sexual sins, alcohol, drugs, envy, hate, pride, murder, jealousy, theft, and such abuses are not options on the Bethlehem road and should be left in Moab. Lightening the load on life's journey is refusing to go back to our baggage left behind in Moab.

I've witnessed souls fleeing Moab, laden with luggage that shouldn't be on the journey. It's dragged along, kicking up dust, making an already difficult journey arduous for the bearer and the brethren beside them. These are the ones who murmur during the dry times and complain at every hill or valley approached. Christ wants you "casting all your care upon Him, for He cares for you" (1 Peter 5:7). He will bury your baggage in the wilderness, if you'll let him.

Ruth was tempted four times with subtle words designed to strike a sensitive cord in her heart for Moab, all to no avail. It's the Lord that tries the heart of man. "The refining pot is for silver and the furnace for gold, but the Lord tests the hearts" (Proverbs 17:3). Ruth was beginning to understand the mortification process. The umbilical cord of Moab has been severed. From this time forward her soul's nourishment will be found in the God of the Hebrews.

Her sister-in-law put her hand to the plough and looked back, making her unfit for the kingdom of God (Luke 9:62). Orpah had second thoughts. Her desire for the gods of Moab outweighed her desire for God and Bethlehem, but not so with Ruth.

"Entreat me not to leave you, or to turn back from following after you." That is to say, I want your presence in my life. I don't want to turn back to Moab. "For wherever you go, I will go."

The afflicting flames Naomi passed through were not sufficient to detour the footsteps of Ruth. Through desert, storm, flame, or flood, she was willing to make the journey to God.

Pick of the Crop: Your sins should not accompany you on your journey. They were severed when you chose Christ as your Lord God and Savior. You must reckon yourself dead to sin but alive to God in Christ Jesus (Romans 6:11). Once the Spirit has made you aware of this unwanted baggage, quickly cast it off, and you'll be freer to express yourself in the praise of the Lord.

20 The Desire of Her Heart

"And wherever you lodge, I will lodge; your people shall be my people, and your God, my God." Ruth 1:16

Ruth delighted to dwell with Naomi, and if her mother-in-law had no place to lay her head, you'd find Ruth there too. Her desire was to fellowship together in unity with God's people.

The God that dwelled in Naomi, Ruth wanted to know more fully. She didn't want to cease from following after Him. She desired to go where He went, to dwell where He dwelled, and to live with Him and His people. She desired all there was of Naomi's God. Ruth was in love. She'd opened her heart, soul, mind, and strength to the control of the Creator of heaven and earth.

"Where you die, I will die, and there will I be buried" (Ruth 1:17). Ruth understood the fleeting flesh. She knew all of life's struggles would cease. Now that she was a child of the kingdom of God, only deeds of service for God would last. The final appointment for the flesh was the grave. There it would be covered and concealed. All its works would decay swiftly. Ruth's will was fixed. Only death would separate these two women.

Death is the great divider. Your spirit returns to God, separating from flesh, that is but dust. "Then the dust will return to the earth as it was, and the spirit will return to God who gave it" (Ecclesiastes 12:7). The true you, an eternal living soul, will be found in Gehenna or glory (Genesis 2:7; Matthew 10:28; John 14:2–3).

Ruth's search for God in the gods of Moab did not satisfy, for all humanity is in search of satisfaction—it's a part of our makeup. Mankind seeks to worship someone or something whether we understand it or not. It's innate; there's no escaping it.

A bee desires nothing more than the sweet nectar of spring's blossom. The deer pants for the water streams, and the soul longing for God is satisfied when it appears before Him (Psalm 42:1–2). God was the desire of Ruth's heart, and nothing short of God would completely satisfy her.

Another decisive divide comes when Bethlehem is our destination. Behold here the trinity of all mankind: spirit, soul and flesh. Naomi represents the spirit returning to God, Ruth represents the soul thirsting for God, and Orpah represents the flesh fleeing God.

Pick of the Crop: Do you want more of God? Is your heart soft and pliable as a lump of clay in His hands? If this is true, He'll give you the desires of your heart (Psalm 37:4). Delighting yourself in God softens the hardest of hearts, preparing those who will for His service. You'll find your sincere desires are solely found in the Savior.

21 Welcoming the Hardships

"When she saw that she was determined to go with her, she stopped speaking to her." Ruth 1:18

Cease from speaking any further on this matter of returning back to Moab and hold back your tongue, Naomi. "To a hungry soul every bitter thing is sweet" (Proverbs 27:7). It's a wonderful work to witness the Spirit of God advancing the soul through adversities.

Welcoming hardships for the gospel of Christ and living a life holy to God comes at a price. Three Jewish young men knew in their collective hearts that taking a stand for God would invite hardship in the wicked society where they lived.

When the king of Babylon wanted to be worshiped as a god, the three men refused. The king became enraged and threaten to cast them into a fiery furnace. The three said to the king, "We don't have to defend ourselves. Our God can save us from you and the flames. But if not let it be known we will not serve you nor your gods."

The king had the men bound with cords and threw them into the flames. And in the midst of the furnace, our Savior, the Son of God, was there to see them through.

The men came out of the fire, free from the cords that had bound them. The fire did not have power over them. The hairs on their heads were not singed. Their coats did not change nor did they smell of smoke (Daniel 3).

Hardships are a way of life in this world. You can experience them alone or with an enduring friend, the Son of God. Ruth was tenacious.

She took a stand and with that decision God would see her through the midst of her fiery trials.

The bitter death of her husband and the sour sum of no offspring may have left a tart taste on the palate of Ruth's heart, but you'd never know it. She didn't shake her fist at God, nor did she murmur. She gladly digested her portion as a necessity on the road to God. Her mature heart accepted this marvelous march all at the hands of the Messiah, recognizing His working in our lives for our good.

A seed laid to rest in the earth breaks through the hard soil to newness of life. If the seed fails or sits still, fearful of the challenge, it will remain buried. Adversities strengthen the children of God, preparing them for the work of God. "For our light affliction, which is but for a moment, is working for us a far more exceeding and eternal weight of glory" (2 Corinthians 4:17).

Agabus, a prophet, told the apostle Paul he would be bound and turned over to the hands of the Gentiles (Acts 21:10–14). Paul welcomed the bitter thoughts of those words as a sweet opportunity to suffer and die for Christ. Agabus couldn't sway Paul from his journey, nor could Naomi sway Ruth from hers.

Pick of the Crop: Like shaping a sword on an anvil or cutting a rough diamond into a beautiful gem, difficulties are used to sharpen the saints for the battle, causing us to sparkle among the stony hearts in this world.

YOUR THOUGHTS

22 THE WILDERNESS

"Now the two of them went until they came to Bethlehem. And it happened, when they had come to Bethlehem, that all the city was excited because of them; and the women said, 'Is this Naomi?'" Ruth 1:19

You're either in the will of God or out; you're for God or against Him. "He who is not with Me is against Me, and he who does not gather with Me scatters abroad" (Matthew 12:30). Far from Bethlehem, the streets of Moab are broad, where the cliché of the day is, "If everyone's doing it, it's okay." Fools, morality by majority is insanity!

In the wilderness, there's the path leading to Bethlehem. It's a road less traveled. The lights and sounds of Moab overshadow that path; it's a wonder how anyone finds it. All who travel that way say there is a lure pulling on their hearts, a longing in their souls that is never satisfied. The world will never be capable of satisfying the souls of men and women. That's one reason why it keeps its occupants in a continual search for the next fleeting fad.

Three women were seen heading out Bethlehem's way. One turned back to Moab's bustling roads and was quickly engulfed, never to be seen nor heard of again.

The citizens of Moab have a secret. The laws of the true God are written on their hearts. "For when Gentiles, who do not have the law, by nature do the things in the law, these, although not having the law, are a law to themselves, who show the work of the law written in their hearts, their conscience also bearing witness, and between themselves their thoughts accusing or else excusing them" (Romans 2:14–15). If God is spoken of in Moab, His Word is frequently mixed with the philosophy of Moab. The music of Moab praises its current culture. The pleasures of Moab are insidious, destroying younger and younger generations.

Poor parenting hand-in-hand with laxity of law threatens Moab's existence. Adultery, fornication, murder, and divorce are paraded. They are the way of Moab. Pride and arrogance are their banners.

This lifestyle does not go unnoticed. God sees their celebrating and testifies against them, "Give wings to Moab, that she may flee and get away; for her cities shall be desolate, without any to dwell in them" (Jeremiah 48:9).

Naomi and Ruth continued their press toward Bethlehem. The pace was slow and steady, a daily walk with many valleys and narrow passes sprinkled along the way. Naomi is a picture of Israel and Ruth the Church, everyday moving closer to a divine union with Yahweh in the Promised Land. Moab faded, and it was a quiet way to Bethlehem as both women reflected on their lives and what may lie ahead.

This was a dangerous time for the two, alone in the wilderness. It's only by God's grace they didn't fall into the hands of thieves, murderers, slave traders, or other enemies of the Hebrews. We're told, "The angel of the Lord encamps all around those who fear Him and delivers them" (Psalm 34:7). We are heavily protected on our daily journey.

Freed from the vices of Moab, the soul must pass through the wilderness, a wasteland as far as the eye can see. It's unfamiliar territory and frightful. The same holds true with the nation of Israel. After leaving Egypt, God led His people "through the wilderness, through a land of deserts and pits, through a land of drought and the shadow of death, through a land that no one crossed and where no one dwelt" (Jeremiah 2:6). The called of God are led through their wilderness experience "to humble you and test you, to know what was in your heart, whether you would keep His commandments or not" (Deuteronomy 8:2).

Pick of the Crop: God sends His people through the wilderness, those arid areas of our lives where time appears to pause. You may say, "The wilderness is an odd place to be led of God." On closer examination you'll discover that the wilderness is a training ground for God's chosen, a place where you'll experience an entirely new realm in Him. In the barren days of the Hebrew nation, they witnessed the striking of the rock Horeb (Exodus 17:6), and they drank the water that freely flowed from that rock. Even so, Christ is found on our wilderness journey, smitten for you and me, by which He provides our spiritual drink in a drought (1 Corinthians 10:4).

23 THE WAY OUT OF THE WILDERNESS

The wilderness is where perseverance is proven, faith is fixed, and patience is preserved in the hope of God. God carried His people through the wilderness as a father carries a son: "In the wilderness where you saw how the Lord your God carried you, as a man carries his son, in all the way that you went until you came to this place'" (Deuteronomy 1:31). Would we expect any less of a deliverance with Naomi and Ruth on their wilderness experience?

Joseph, son of Jacob, began his wilderness experience cast into a pit by his brothers, sold as a slave, and carried down into Egypt (Genesis 37:22–28). David's wilderness experience was fleeing King Saul and the army of Israel (1 Samuel 24:1–2). Elijah the prophet went through his wilderness experience fleeing Jezebel, wife of King Ahab (1 Kings 19:1–4).

Your length of stay in the wilderness may be forty days, four weeks, or forty years. Time or distance is not our concern. We are commanded to simply endure. "Run with patience the race that is set before us" (Hebrews 12:1). Nevertheless, an extended stay in the wilderness can be brought about by our disobedience.

All of the successes below were completed on the other side of their wilderness experience. Joseph's life saved many lives: "But as for you, you meant evil against me; *but* God meant it for good, in order to bring it about as *it is* this day, to save many people alive" (Genesis 50:20). David ruled a kingdom: "Therefore all the elders of Israel came to the king at Hebron, and King David made a covenant with them at Hebron before the Lord. And they anointed David king over Israel" (2 Samuel 5:3). Elijah was ushered to heaven in a chariot of fire: "Then it happened, as they continued on and talked, that suddenly a chariot of fire appeared with horses of fire, and separated the two of them; and Elijah went up by a whirlwind into heaven" (2 Kings 2:11). Only God knows the exploits that are waiting on the other side of our wilderness experience.

Our Lord "was led by the Spirit into the wilderness, being tempted for forty days by the devil" (Luke 4:1–2). Christ both sympathized and empathized with the weakness of our humanity. He was in the wilderness wrestling with the devil and triumphed, leaving us an example. Notice the wilderness is not a place of permanent dwelling but your preparation for a work of God.

The shortest distance out of the wilderness of Moab to Bethlehem will be to travel west past Mount Nebo, where Moses viewed the Promised Land from the top of Pisgah (a cleft or division in the mountain), and died (Deuteronomy 32:48–50, 34:1–5). Pisgah is toward the Jordan River, which is north of the Dead Sea. Israel's final days of their forty year wilderness wanderings were spent in Moab, east of the Jordan River near the city of Jericho. "Then the children of Israel moved, and camped in the plains of Moab on the side of the Jordan across from Jericho" (Numbers 22:1).

The way out of Moab will usher Naomi and Ruth into God's Promised Land by the same path at the same time of year the nation of Israel left Moab under the direction of God in prior years. Recall when Israel as a nation crossed the Jordan River: "As those who bore the ark came to the Jordan, and the feet of the priests who bore the ark dipped in the edge of the water (for the Jordan overflows all its banks during the whole time of harvest)" (Joshua 3:15).

Passing Mount Nebo, our travelers crossed the Jordan River, that great demarcation of the desert separating God's promises from the wilderness. Jordan means "to descend or go down"—literally, to descend down into judgment. Jesus was baptized in this same Jordan River (Matthew 3:13), likely in the same location where Israel, Naomi, and Ruth crossed into the Promised Land. The Jordan River empties into the Dead Sea. Before entering into the Promised Land, they had to pass the junction of humility, where death and dying meet. It's the last step in the wilderness of Moab.

Life should be lived preparing to die, which precedes the promise of eternal life. Death and life, sunrise, sunset, rain, drought, sowing, reaping, night, day, sleep, and awakenings—all are a part of the cycle of life. Although their actual crossing isn't recorded, God's record stands sure. He had already shown them the way out of Moab (Joshua 3:14–17).

The water of the wilderness met my needs.
The deluge in the desert rescued me.
The dayspring on high answered my cry,
Whereby I revived when He drew nigh.

Pick of the Crop: God has appointed a set time and path for your exodus out of the wilderness, marked by the heights of Pisgah and the depths of the Jordan River. There is a renewed, victorious life in the promises of God waiting for you on the other side of your wilderness journey.

24 The Promised Land

With Moab behind, the Promised Land before and God in their midst, it was a lovely life.

Free from a land I grew to know
of pain, sorrows, and spirits bowed.
Days and nights both tell the toll,
Sin's stains plowed through my soul.
Through desert lands I journeyed slow.
Spirit within, cease not to blow
To the Land of Goldenglow.
Lord, to Thee my life I owe.
Peaceful land, I'll come and grow,
In love and grace my life will show.
Christ within was heaven sown
Fill me up and make me whole.

All who are called out of the world, out of Moab, pass these spiritual landmarks on their journey to a closer walk with God. The wilderness is a testing ground for trying your love for God. Mount Nebo/Pisgah speaks of a heightened sense of separating ourselves from the former life while looking forward by faith to the promises of God. The Jordan River crossing speaks of baptism by faith, having our dead works carried away by the currents of the Creator and released into the Dead Sea. Our resurrected life begins by crossing into the Promised Land of God.

At this point in their journey, Naomi may have shared with Ruth the story of how God divided the Jordan River to allow the entire nation of Israel access into the Promised Land on dry ground (Joshua 3:14–4:18). Moses desperately wanted to enter this land in his flesh, but God prevented him (Deuteronomy 3:25–26). Better yet, Moses appeared with Elijah in the spirit before the glory of the incarnate Christ within the Promised Land (Matthew 17:1–3). Moses' desires were fulfilled beyond his expectation, his wilderness trials trumped in God permitting His servant entrance into the land after his flesh was dead.

Do you see the beauty of the promise God has for you? Are you eager to possess those promises? Is your flesh out of the way? No one can fully enjoy what God has in store as long as the flesh is flourishing. Be assured those fleshly desires will keep you from God's promises.

Pick of the Crop: "For all the promises of God in Him are Yes, and in Him Amen, to the glory of God through us" (2 Corinthians 1:20). All that God has ever promised is completely fulfilled in His Son, Christ Jesus our Lord. His promises offer hope in Him to perform His Word. Returning to the Promised Land for Naomi was literally returning to all God had promised her, her family and her people. If you're living outside of what our Lord has promised you, repent and return to Him. He will accept you with open arms back into all goodness. Return now without delay.

25 JERICHO

Naomi and Ruth would have passed south of Jericho the first major victory in the Israelites' conquest of Canaan (Joshua 6). Another opportunity for Naomi to share the mighty works of God with Ruth.

Jericho had built a formidable wall around the city to shield them from attack, but that wall became feeble before those who followed the ways of God. At His command, the wall fell—a lesson to all who delight to enter into God's promises. The walls we all have manufactured to protect ourselves, to hide the works of the flesh, must fall to the power of God.

It's unreasonable to believe the walls we've built would remain within the promises of God, and yet there are those who continue to seek refuge behind the façade they have fashioned. There were other battles to be fought within the Promised Land, but those victories could not be won until the walls of our making were overthrown.

The things God destroys in you are not to be rebuilt. "For if I build again those things which I destroyed, I make myself a transgressor" (Galatians 2:18). Don't willfully sin against God, who has saved you. As a dog returns to its vomit and a pig to the mud from which it was cleansed (2 Peter 2:22), so is the one who rebuilds the walls in their life to conceal the sin within their heart.

It was here at the city of Jericho, Joshua (whose name means "Jehovah has saved") saved a lone prostitute and her entire family because she believed the call of God on her life (Joshua 6:25, Hebrews 11:31). She was Israel's convert in Canaan.

The terrain was noticeably changing from that of the Jordan River Valley. They were traveling up and down over a seemingly endless melody of rolling hills. Fig trees and vineyards were multiplying. The land smelled of fields which the Lord had blessed. Finally, Bethlehem was in view, and it was altogether lovely.

Pick of the Crop: Creating walls is a trait that began in the garden. These walls are skillfully crafted within our imaginations to protect us from the onslaught of the world. All the while, these walls prevent God from entering in and reigning within us. Over time we put great faith in our walls, while God is waiting to be our fortress. Let your walls fall before God, and watch Him shield you with His love.

26 Bethlehem

Within the walls of Bethlehem secured and free,
My soul attests, t'was Heaven's best;
He came and pardoned me.

Never stop short of your call. Life is precious. You have worth in Christ. God has paid a great price for you, and He loves you. "For I know the thoughts that I think toward you, says the Lord, thoughts of peace and not of evil, to give you a future and a hope" (Jeremiah 29:11). Your true fulfillment in life with God is never accomplished living outside of Bethlehem, outside of the will of God.

Within Bethlehem you're part of the body of Christ. You're a member of an active, functional, and living spiritual body. Your existence is to live for Christ and aid in the ministry of His spiritual body on earth. "For as the body is one and has many members, but all the members of that one body, being many, are one body, so also is Christ. For by one Spirit we were all baptized into one body—whether Jews or Greeks, whether slaves or free—and have all been made to drink into one Spirit" (1 Corinthians 12:12–13).

Everyone has his or her role in the body of Christ. If you're a foot, don't forsake the head, and if you're the head, don't forfeit the feet. The feet are your supporters, your rarely seen base. Without them where would you be? Without the head, there would be no decisions, no vision.

We all have significance in Christ. Ruth would learn to live and work together with the Hebrew people with one common goal, service to God and care for one another, "that there should be no schism in the body, but that the members should have the same care for one another" (1 Corinthians 12:25).

Bethlehem is where the anointed king-shepherd boy would feed his father's sheep (1 Samuel 17:15). It's where a chorus of shepherds would one day come to see the Chief Shepherd boy lying in a manger, and they would go out, proclaiming His glory (Luke 2:15–18). Beautiful Bethlehem would be known as the city of David, and many in Israel would understand what Scripture said: Christ would come of the seed of David and from the town where David lived (John 7:42).

They reached Bethlehem, but there were many more lessons to learn—lessons on how to conduct oneself within the new sanctified life—a life to be lived in this world, but not of the world, a life that is both distant and different from the life of Moab.

Pick of the Crop:

The nations cheer Vanity Fair
All together cannot compare.
You alone became the host
To Messiah's birth; in that you'll boast.

Christ was born in Bethlehem and would like to be born in you. You have been called to share in the Bread of Life with the people of that city. Fellowship with the Saints builds us up in holy faith. Become a partaker of Bethlehem's Bread today and live.

27 WANDERING FROM BETHLEHEM

"All the city was excited because of them; and the women said, 'Is this Naomi?'" Ruth 1:19

The inhabitants of Bethlehem were perplexed, uneasy about these two, especially because of Naomi's transformation. Her appearance had changed, her pleasant ways spent. What happened?

What bundles of burdens we fall under when wandering from Bethlehem. We get lost in our ways, becoming slack in our devotion to the call of Christ. We give place to the devil, and he squanders our testimony in an attempt to kill us. Keep this in heart, dear saints: **the devil hates you!** "Be sober, be vigilant; because your adversary the devil walks about like a roaring lion, seeking whom he may devour" (1 Peter 5:8). Sheep in the center of the sheepfold are safer. The devil's waiting for you to wander away from God's barrier of protection. Beloved, make your way to the center of God's will for you and there remain.

The mighty Samson, which means "sunlight," shone bright and strong in the service of God but waned as a wimp among women. He moved closer and closer to the boundaries of God's protective barrier, until finally he crossed over, removing himself from the source of the light that was within, that is, the light of God. He had made a vow for the service of the Almighty, but gradually his pride, self-will, disobedience, and lust for women weakened his walk and caused his fall.

God had mercy and grace on Samson after losing his sight and strength. He was lifted after his humiliation. He received spiritual insight at the loss of worldly vision and took on renewed spiritual power when his desire for this world ceased. All our foolish pain and suffering may have been avoidable had we simply remained in the midst of God's sheepfold. The love of God blessed Samson's final days by avenging his enemies and giving him a name in the Hall of Faith. (Judges 13–16, Hebrews 11:32).

God delighted to bless the later life of Naomi by forgetting her past, giving her spiritual insights, strength to see past her circumstances and to hope in her God. Naomi had returned to the center of God's will for her.

Pick of the Crop: When Naomi wandered from Bethlehem, she became emaciated and lost ten years living in Moab. The dangers of wandering away from the securities of God may someday cost you your life or the lives of the ones you love. Don't wander away from Christ Jesus who loves you. Wandering begins in your imagination, and then your motives shift, and finally your actions move you away from Christ. Don't let your wandering imagination separate you from God in Christ. Pray to Christ for strength to keep your mind stayed on Him and Him alone.

28 Bitterness Blinds

"But she said to them, 'Do not call me Naomi; call me Mara, for the Almighty has dealt very bitterly with me. I went out full, and the Lord has brought me home again empty. Why do you call me Naomi, since the Lord has testified against me, and the Almighty has afflicted me?'" Ruth 1:20–21

Naomi's testimony was tarnished; there was no joy in her soul. She attributed this to the hand of the Almighty, and for that, she was bitter. She testified, "I'm not better, but bitter over my losses." Woe to angry, bitter women. In stoutness of heart, they boast, "I went out full. I went out from the comforts of God with plenty." The security of marriage and children exalts the self. Financial blessings elevate ego. Woe to the bitter women in the body of Christ. They threaten to disrupt the tender growth of proselytes by their tongues. May they hearken unto the voice of our Lord and hold their peace.

The Israelites traveled a three-day journey into the wilderness beyond Egypt and found no clean water to drink. What water they did find tasted bitter, so they complained to Moses. When Moses cast a tree in the bitter water at the direction of the Lord, the water became sweet (Exodus 15:22–25). Christ cast His tree into the bitter pool of our sinful lives. That tree was His cross, turning life's bitter consumption sweet.

The same God who called Naomi back to Bethlehem called the Israelites out of Egypt. The same God who saved Naomi's life saved the life of that great nation. How many of us, like Naomi and Israel, murmur and complain when bitter circumstances surround us like a pool of water? Bitter marriages, families, employment, housing, health, finances, and losses will leave us bitter. Don't lose sight of what God has done. Don't lose heart in the hope of what He promises to do in our lives. Naomi was home, but she was neither hopeful nor happy about her future.

Pick of the Crop: When Christ begins to take away, our eyes are keenly focused on the things He is removing, and we miss the greater picture. Our self-life creates a bitter heart, preventing us from seeing the work of God. Pray to Christ to remove our bitter hearts that we might see His wonderful working in our lives.

29 Empty of Ourselves

"The Lord has brought me home again empty." Ruth 1:21

Notice how quickly Naomi ignored Ruth, who had endured similar losses and had forsaken all to follow the God of the Hebrews. She forgot about the friend that had traveled through the wilderness with her, passing Mount Nebo and crossing the Jordan into the Promised Land with her on the road to Bethlehem. Now a spirit of bitterness would not allow her to acknowledge the hand of God that saved her from complete abandonment. God is able to create a blessing out of our disobedience. Naomi did not return to Bethlehem empty. She returned with Ruth, her friend and daughter, and it was the love of the Father who brought her home again.

Naomi went out full of her own accomplishments. Now that she was home, obedient to the call of God, He could accomplish His work within her heart, but she must first be emptied so none other than God may be glorified. Our blessed Messiah empties His vessels of their selfish pride in order to fill them with the love of His Spirit, and we in turn pour out the love of Christ into other vessels.

There was a woman, similar to our sister Naomi, whose husband died, leaving her in debt. This woman also had two sons and was in jeopardy of losing them as slaves to a creditor. The widow cried out to God within the prophet Elisha ("God of supplication"), and God harkened to her plea. The prophet asked what she had in her home. She said she had nothing except a jar of oil, that is, a flask of anointing oil. He told her to borrow as many empty vessels as she could from her neighbors and pour into those vessels all of the oil she had.

She did according to the Word of God through the prophet, pouring the little anointing oil she had into the empty vessels. By the working of God, her oil multiplied as she poured it into the vessels. When all of them had been filled, the oil ceased from flowing. Elisha told her to go sell the oil to pay her debt and live on the rest (2 Kings 4:1–7). A mysterious way was made for a debt she could not pay. God's method of multiplying is past finding out.

When God's emptying process is complete, He leaves the willing soul with nothing of self-accomplishments. All we have of eternal value is from His anointing, to be poured into the lives of others. Naomi, having been emptied, would begin to receive God's anointing for this purpose in her life, to be poured into the heart of Ruth, another vessel that had been emptied and prepared to receive the things of God.

Pick of the Crop: Selfish desires hinder spiritual advancement. A vessel full of self cannot coexist in a vessel full of the Spirit of God. The more self is eliminated from our lives the greater the ground the Spirit of God can occupy. Denying yourself of the things that displease God is a step in the direction of emptying yourself of this world.

30 New Season

"So Naomi returned, and Ruth the Moabitess her daughter-in-law with her, who returned from the country of Moab. Now they came to Bethlehem at the beginning of barley harvest." Ruth 1:22

It was a new season in the life of these two. "For lo the winter is past, the rain is over and gone. The flowers appear on the earth; the time of singing of birds has come, and the voice of the turtledove is heard in our land. The fig tree puts forth her green figs, and the vines with the tender grapes give a good smell…" (Song of Solomon 2:11–13). Their time in Moab had come to an end.

The day of salvation is a memorial to be celebrated, when God delivered you and saved you out of the bondage of this world. Naomi and Ruth had been delivered from Moab, entering into Bethlehem at the beginning of barley harvest. It was springtime in the month the ancient Hebrews called Abib. "You shall keep the Feast of Unleavened Bread (you shall eat unleavened bread seven days, as I commanded you, at the time appointed in the month of Abib, for in it you came out of Egypt; none shall appear before Me empty)" (Exodus 23:15). To those in the western world, this was mid-March through April.

The beginning of barley harvest is a special time for the nation of Israel, and it will be for Naomi and Ruth a memorial day. It was at this time in former years that Israel first celebrated their Passover Feast and the Feast of Unleavened Bread while being released from the bondage of Egypt. "And Moses said to the people: 'Remember this day in which you went out of Egypt, out of the house of bondage; for by strength of hand the Lord brought you out of this place. No leavened bread shall be eaten. On this day you are going out, in the month Abib'" (Exodus 13:3–4).

And it was at this same time of the year in their far future that our Lord was crucified. "On the fourteenth day of the first month at twilight is the Lord's Passover" (Leviticus 23:5). The feast of unleavened bread was the Passover (Luke 22:1). Our Lord, King Jesus, was presented before His people on that day to be slain. "Now it was the Preparation Day of the Passover, and about the sixth hour. And he said to the Jews, 'Behold your King!'" (John 19:14).

Can you see the crop with the eye of your imagination, those glistening, golden stocks reaching toward heaven, waving in the wind as an offering to God? It's God who supplies the sun, rain, and earth that they might ripen and grow.

> "He causes the grass to grow for the cattle,
> And vegetation for the service of man,
> That he may bring forth food from the earth."
> (Psalm 104:14)

Bethlehem rejoiced at this time: "They rejoice before You according to the joy of harvest" (Isaiah 9:3). There was no noticeable rejoicing in Moab between our duo. Troubled tears flowed as a mighty river. Tears were sown in the soil with little results. But behold, it was a new season, and in Bethlehem there was rejoicing.

There are many tearful times in this life under the sun as we sow into the lives of others and trust God with those things that are precious to us. There are those days you may feel as if you gave your all to mend a marriage, to save a son, or deliver a daughter. You fervently tried to foster a failing friendship, and uncontrollable tears sprang up from within. Am I sowing in vain? To what purpose do I continue?

Those who sow in tears
Shall reap in joy.
He who continually goes forth weeping,
Bearing seed for sowing,
Shall doubtless come again with rejoicing,
Bringing his sheaves with him.
(Psalm 126:5–6)

The day's coming when we will rejoice in what God has done. Our tears will be turned to joy, the longing of our heart will be turned to laughter. It was the beginning of barley harvest for Naomi and Ruth, and they would reap the benefits.

How wonderful of God to save Ruth and place her in the best place to grow, at the "beginning of barley harvest." There was a joyful celebration unlike any she'd experienced in Moab. Celebration centered on the feasts. These events pointed to the Messiah, the Lamb of God, Jesus Christ our righteousness. He willingly gave His life as a sacrificial lamb—God's perfect, spotless, acceptable lamb. "God will provide for Himself the lamb for a burnt offering" (Genesis 22:8).

Thank God for the changing of the seasons! For Naomi and Ruth, the rain and dark clouds of despair had passed and a time of celebration was at hand. As the Earth journeys through its seasons, so too does every man, woman, boy, and girl. If you understand the seasons, you'll understand the times, if you're not hypocritical of heart (Luke 12:56).

Fragrant flowers fill the air.
Winter trees no longer bare.
Shorn bark behold God's light.
It's a new season from tomb to life.

Days of gray cease to blast.
Death succumbed, colored fields contrast
the warp and woof of seasons past
and shout for joy, "It's spring at last!"

Pick of the Crop: If you've recently come forth out of Moab and have given your life to Christ, it's a new season for you. Expect to see the new fruits of righteousness sprouting within your heart as you grow in the grace and knowledge of our Lord.

31 The Feast of Passover (Pesach)

"On the fourteenth day of the first month at twilight is the Lord's Passover" (Leviticus 23:5). The Feast of Passover marks the evening when the spotless, sacrificial lamb was slain, and throughout that night and into the day, Israel was delivered out of bondage from their enemy. "And I delivered you out of the hand of the Egyptians and out of the hand of all who oppressed you" (Judges 6:9).

Ruth would have learned that on the night prior to Israel's departure out of slavery, each family was commanded to kill a one-year-old lamb without spot or blemish. They were instructed to put the blood of that lamb on the sides and upper doorposts of their homes. When the plague of death passed through Egypt that night, all the firstborn who were sheltered in a home whose doorposts were covered by the blood of the lamb lived. If your choice was contrary to the command of God, death found you (Exodus 12:1–14).

"Christ, our Passover, was sacrificed for us" (1 Corinthians 5:7). When salvation came by accepting Christ into our life, we were delivered out of the bondage of sin. Christ in us made it possible to flee Egypt, which represents the sinful life of bondage in this world. Most importantly, our soul will not see the plague of death. We've been covered, sealed by the blood of the Lamb upon the doorpost of our heart. In the Feast of Passover, that sacrificial lamb represented Christ, and He alone liberates the soul from sin's shackles.

Messiah's manner, mourning and myrrh.
Managed His cross, marred for morgue.
Might made clear, mount off death's floor.

Seated in majesty, His blood implores.
Remove mire of mind, may I wholly be thine.
Mine to possess and I'll see thee on high.

Pick of the Crop: Salvation is the first step out of the slavery of sin. The deliverance of your soul is only possible by accepting the Passover Lamb, Jesus Christ. Asking Jesus to live in you is spiritually partaking of the Passover Feast. Come eat of this feast until your soul is satisfied.

32 THE FEAST OF UNLEAVENED BREAD (CHAG HAMOTZI)

The Feast of Unleavened Bread came the following day. "And on the fifteenth day of the same month is the Feast of Unleavened Bread to the Lord; seven days you must eat unleavened bread" (Leviticus 23:6).

Leaven (yeast) in most cases symbolizes sin and pride exalting itself against the knowledge of God. Bread will rise with a hint of leaven. Bread without leaven will not rise but will lie flat. So too Christ, the Bread of Life, was laid in the grave during the Feast of Unleavened Bread, a feast which speaks of the sinless life of Christ and of His burial. Christ was leaven free "who committed no sin, nor was deceit found in His mouth" (1 Peter 2:22).

Ruth learned this memorial was observed for seven days. The people were to search their homes to remove all leaven. Their houses were to be completely leaven free, and for seven days they were to eat unleavened bread (Exodus 12:15–20).

Jesus warned, "Take heed and beware of the leaven of the Pharisees and the Sadducees" (Matthew 16:6). The Pharisees and Sadducees were religious rulers practicing sinful, pride-filled acts. Imagine how one small doctrinal error quickly ferments throughout the faith. The practice of a lifestyle free from sin, which puts to death the desires of their flesh, didn't exist in them.

"A little leaven leavens the whole lump" (Galatians 5:9). As the people of Israel diligently searched their homes to remove the leaven, we are to search our hearts, daily removing any indication of sin in our lives. The cleansing blood of Christ has made it possible to practice a life free of sin.

A life lived with Christ is a life of purity, unspotted from the world. We are encouraged to "keep the feast, not with old leaven, nor with the leaven of malice and wickedness, but with the unleavened bread of sincerity and truth" (1 Corinthians 5:8). This was Ruth's way of life.

Pick of the Crop: After salvation we are immediately empowered to live a life without sin. We are instructed to diligently search our hearts, removing the sin of malice and impure thoughts. Should the deeds of dead works return, we learn to cry out to God:

> Search me, O God, and know my heart;
> Try me, and know my anxieties;
> And see if there is any wicked way in me,
> And lead me in the way everlasting. (Psalm 139:23–24)

33 Feast of Firstfruits (Yom Habikkurim)

"Speak to the children of Israel, and say to them: 'When you come into the land which I give to you, and reap its harvest, then you shall bring a sheaf of the firstfruits of your harvest to the priest. He shall wave the sheaf before the Lord, to be accepted on your behalf; on the day after the Sabbath the priest shall wave it'" (Leviticus 23:10–11). This feast came three days after the Passover. The first of the harvested fruit were given to the priest to offer up to the Lord as a wave offering. He would lift it up and wave the first of the harvest in the air.

This feast speaks of the resurrection of Jesus Christ three days after the Passover. Christ bore our sins, though He Himself did not sin, and as a result death had no claim on Him. The resurrection of Jesus teaches there is a new way of life, a new resurrected life. "But now Christ is risen from the dead, and has become the firstfruits of those who have fallen asleep. For since by man came death, by Man also came the resurrection of the dead. For as in Adam all die, even so in Christ all shall be made alive. But each one in his own order: Christ the firstfruits, afterward those who are Christ's at His coming" (1 Corinthians 15:20–23).

In nature, fall and winter blow in their changes over the fields. They are cold, barren, and lifeless to the naked eye, but all the while life is germinating under the soil where seeds were laid to rest. Spring arises, and the fields demonstrate the resurrected life of seeds in their glory. "Except a corn of wheat fall into the ground and die, it abideth alone: but if it die, it bringeth forth much fruit" (John 12:24 KJV).

Death's door opens to life. Dying to our ego, our pride, and anything that exalts the life of self must be met. When we have died to our selfish ways of living, the new fruits of a godly way of life are clearly seen. This was the life demonstrated in Ruth.

Pick of the Crop: Christ Jesus rose from the dead three days after His death to become the first-fruit of many to come. We are to live a new life in Christ in this present moment. You are spiritually resurrected with Christ, free from former works of the flesh. This day, begin to celebrate your new resurrected life in all that you do, giving glory to God for His son who saved you.

34 Feast of Weeks or Pentecost (Shavu'ot)

The people were to count seven weeks and celebrate the Feast of Weeks (Deuteronomy 16: 9–12). That's fifty days after the Feast of Firstfruits. "And you shall count for yourselves from the day after the Sabbath, from the day that you brought the sheaf of the wave offering: seven Sabbaths shall be completed. Count fifty days to the day after the seventh Sabbath; then you shall offer a new grain offering to the Lord" (Leviticus 23:15–16). This feast is also known as Pentecost (Acts 2:1). The word *pentecost* means fiftieth day.

Strangers, that is to say the foreigners, were invited to participate in the celebration. "You shall rejoice before the Lord your God, you and your son and your daughter, your male servant and your female servant, the Levite who is within your gates, the stranger and the fatherless and the widow who are among you, at the place where the Lord your God chooses to make His name abide" (Deuteronomy 16:11). Can you envision Ruth as a willing participant in the ceremony of God with both Jew and Gentile rejoicing together as one?

Pentecost points to the third person in the Godhead, the Holy Spirit. The Holy Spirit teaches the people of God, bringing practical, spiritual lessons to our minds. "But the Comforter, which is the Holy Ghost, whom the Father will send in my name, he shall teach you all things, and bring all things to your remembrance, whatsoever I have said unto you" (John 14:26 KJV).

He is the Spirit of the Lord who brings liberty to the people of God. "Now the Lord is the Spirit; and where the Spirit of the Lord is, there is liberty" (2 Corinthians 3:17). He is the Spirit of Truth. "He will guide you into all truth; for He will not speak on His own authority, but whatever He hears He will speak; and He will tell you things to come" (John 16:13).

"When the Day of Pentecost had fully come, they were all with one accord in one place" (Acts 2:1). It's a beautiful thing to witness God's people all with one mind in one place in anticipation of the Spirit. We are now strengthened with might from within so that we might be filled with the fullness of God. (Ephesians 3:16–19). Power to deny the world, the flesh, and the devil. Power over fear, doubt, and unbelief. Power from inside to make a difference in the lives of lost souls in the world around us. Hallelujah! In the crucifixion year of Christ, fifty days after the Feast of Firstfruits during the summer time, the Holy Spirit was freely given. Pentecost indeed had fully come. It is wonderful to consider that during the same time of the year in the life of Moses the Ten Commandments were also freely given (Exodus 19–20).

Pick of the Crop: The Holy Spirit of God has fully come to help us in our infirmities and weaknesses. We have living power within our lives to live a holy life pleasing to God and man. We have been given power within to tell the deeds of the flesh, "No," while saying, "Yes," to the Spirit of God.

35 The Feast of Trumpets (Rosh Hashanah)

"Speak to the children of Israel, saying: 'In the seventh month, on the first day of the month, you shall have a sabbath-rest, a memorial of blowing of trumpets, a holy convocation. You shall do no customary work on it; and you shall offer an offering made by fire to the Lord'" (Leviticus 23:24–25).

Ruth would have learned that the trumpets sound a call to remember God's awesome presence, striking a fearful cord in their hearts (Exodus 19:16–19). "And so terrifying was the sight that Moses said, 'I am exceedingly afraid and trembling'" (Hebrews 12:21).

The sound of the trumpet announces God's holy intention to judge sin. Today the trumpets declare, "Cry aloud, spare not; lift up your voice like a trumpet; tell My people their transgression, and the house of Jacob their sins" (Isaiah 58:1).

We can't imagine the deep, dark, distant deluge that sin has brought into our lives. Sin has scarred all who ever lived. No weapon, famine, nor pestilence can claim that title. Little is said about this three-letter word in the world today. In some pulpits the word *sin* is a banned word. Identifying our sins touches us deeply, alerting us to a coming judgment.

The world has relabeled sin in an attempt to soften its effects on our consciences. It helps humanity feel freer to continue to do that which is wrong, living in the darkness of the imagination of the heart. We're commanded to cry out against sin while the world seeks to rename it. What God calls sin the world calls sicknesses, but be assured, sin by any name is death. Sin separates man from God, and God will judge all sin.

A cry was heard, a shout rang out, alerting the slumbering hearts of ten virgins. Five were wise and five were foolish. Both groups possessed lamps. The foolish took their lamps without oil. That is to say, they carried an outward expression of faith, "but the wise took oil in their vessels with their lamps."

The call to meet the bridegroom prompted the virgins to awake and trim their lamps. The wise were able to ignite their burning love, passion, and longing for the bridegroom, but the foolish could not. The foolish wanted to ignite their lamps with the oil of the wise, which was an impossibility. You cannot enter into fellowship on the relationship and experience of another. The rapture came and the foolish were locked out, while the wise entered into a sweet fellowship with the bridegroom (Matthew 25:1–13).

The cry to repentance and a call to come to a relationship with Christ is going forth. Awake and respond to the call.

Pick of the Crop: The coming judgment is nearer than when we believe. Will you be ready? The mercies of God are long-suffering in love, but the love of God will ultimately send His judgment against sin. The sound of the trumpets will alert the dull in heart to be prepared. The voice of the trumpets are calling this hour. Will you come? Will you come now?

36 The Day of Atonement (Yom Kippur)

"Also the tenth day of this seventh month shall be the Day of Atonement. It shall be a holy convocation for you; you shall afflict your souls, and offer an offering made by fire to the Lord. And you shall do no work on that same day, for it is the Day of Atonement, to make atonement for you before the Lord your God" (Leviticus 23:27–28).

The Day of Atonement followed ten days after the Feast of Trumpets. To atone is to cover, cancel, cleanse, and restore the people from sin's stains. Ruth would have learned that the cleansing of the people by the high priest was accomplished before the mercy seat of God.

> He shall take some of the blood of the bull and sprinkle it with his finger on the mercy seat on the east side; and before the mercy seat he shall sprinkle some of the blood with his finger seven times. Then he shall kill the goat of the sin offering, which is for the people, bring its blood inside the veil, do with that blood as he did with the blood of the bull, and sprinkle it on the mercy seat and before the mercy seat. (Leviticus 16:14–15)

This was a time of sobriety and self-reflection for the individual and the nation. This feast ushered all who believed into the presence of the awesome, almighty God and His seat of mercy where we are forgiven. Now Jesus Christ is our High Priest of Heaven, ministering before the throne of God continually. "We have such a High Priest, who is seated at the right hand of the throne of the Majesty in the heavens, a Minister of the sanctuary and of the true tabernacle which the Lord erected, and not man" (Hebrews 8:1–2).

> But Christ came as High Priest of the good things to come, with the greater and more perfect tabernacle not made with hands, that is, not of this creation. Not with the blood of goats and calves, but with His own blood He entered the Most Holy Place once for all, having obtained eternal redemption. For if the blood of bulls and goats and the ashes of a heifer, sprinkling the unclean, sanctifies for the purifying of the flesh, how much more shall the blood of Christ, who through the eternal Spirit offered Himself without spot to God, cleanse your conscience from dead works to serve the living God? (Hebrews 9:11–14)

It was the blood of Christ, sprinkled before the Mercy Seat of the Eternal Father, that bought us eternal life. The Day of Atonement is a portrait of our eternal priest. "For Christ has not entered the holy places made with hands, which are copies of the true, but into heaven itself, now to appear in the presence of God for us" (Hebrews 9:24). Christ blotted out the sins of all who would simply believe, a belief demonstrated in word and deeds. You've been made clean. Ruth would have learned God is a merciful God willing to cleanse whosoever will.

Pick of the Crop: The blood of Christ sprinkled on the mercy seat of God covers and cleanses the sins of a multitude. What the blood of goats and calves symbolized in the interim, Christ's blood fixed for the eternal.

37 Feast of Tabernacle (Booths-Sukkot)

Ruth would have learned this feast was a time of rejoicing over the gathering of the crops. It was a time of cancellation of debt at the end of a seven year cycle (Deuteronomy 31:10). A time when men, women, children, and the strangers all gathered together to hear, learn, and fear God by the reading of His Word (Deuteronomy 16:13–16, 31:10–13).

The men were to dwell in booths, tent-like structures, for seven days with celebratory hearts, remembering how God delivered them out of Egypt and kept them through the wilderness when they were living in booths or tabernacles (Leviticus 23:42–43).

Christ, our tabernacle, is a dwelling place from the wilderness of this world. "My tabernacle also shall be with them; indeed I will be their God, and they shall be My people" (Ezekiel 37:27). Ever so true to His Word, God's tabernacle came in the person of Jesus Christ, "Emmanuel, which being interpreted is, God with us" (Matthew 1:23 KJV). He tabernacled among us: "And the Word became flesh and dwelt among us, and we beheld His glory, the glory as of the only begotten of the Father, full of grace and truth" (John 1:14).

Christ is our tabernacle, and we are to abide in Him. "Abide in Me, and I in you. As the branch cannot bear fruit of itself, unless it abides in the vine, neither can you, unless you abide in Me" (John 15:4). Our satisfaction is met in His dwelling, keeping our minds fixed on Him, remembering this—the second coming of Christ is nearer today than when we first believed.

"And I heard a loud voice from heaven saying, 'Behold, the tabernacle of God *is* with men, and He will dwell with them, and they shall be His people. God Himself will be with them and be their God'"

(Revelation 21:3). The new Heaven and Earth are not far off and coming with them is the tabernacle of God, dwelling with His people. All things will be made new. It's an awesome thought to behold. Now come dwell with us!

Pick of the Crop: When Christ is accepted as your new way of life, He is in you and you in Him, living in the unity of the Holy Spirit. As the fish is in the water and the water is in the fish, the greater is the sustainer of the lesser. Further still, in that day you will know that Christ is in the Father and we are in Christ and Christ in us (John 14:20).

38 There's Life in Bethlehem

Again and again we see this pattern repeated for our encouragement. The people of God in this life cry out, and our Lord delivers. Christ can never be exhausted. Through our difficulties, we are to trust in God's delivering power specific for our individual needs. It's a comforting truth to discover Christ was following His people in the wilderness. Their needs were met; they drank during a drought. The same truth can be told in our lives today. Christ is with you presently. He is that unassuming Rock that has never failed, even when we don't see Him.

"Now the Jews' Feast of Tabernacles was at hand. . . . On the last day, that great day of the feast, Jesus stood and cried out, saying, 'If anyone thirsts, let him come to Me and drink. He who believes in Me, as the Scripture has said, out of his heart will flow rivers of living water" (John 7:2, 37–38).

With the above promise, will not the God-man provide a personal tabernacle for all those who thirst?

These are fundamental principles which should always be taught to the novice in the way of holiness. There were multiple festivals throughout the year for Ruth to enjoy besides those mentioned above, festivals and feasts where Ruth would have gleaned spiritual truth about the coming Messiah and His plan for His people and humanity. These were celebrations designed for the people about God, "which are a shadow of things to come, but the substance is of Christ" (Colossians 2:17).

House of bread, in famine led, the hungry hearts,
to you who fed.
Through ages roll, the weary soul, found strength in thee,
from sin and foe.

House of bread, shepherds flocked, to look up on,
    Christ the Rock.
In manger laid, the humbled gazed, that holy child,
    whom God had gave.

O house of bread, my Savior bled, laid down His head,
    the grave His bed.
And devils dread, for Christ has tread, on Satan sway,
    his throne brayed.
House of bread, the Lord's alive! The sting of death,
    stopped not His rise.
Christ seized the prize, passed through the skies,
    to Heaven's abode, glory enthroned.

Pick of the Crop: Life in Bethlehem is exemplified by life. During a famine there was life, and in harvest there was abundant life. The same is true while living in God. Ruth was dead yet made alive, drawn to the center of God's will for her life, lived out in Bethlehem. And some of you were dead in Moab and made alive through the power of God in Christ. Be drawn to Bethlehem, the center of God's will for you. There remain and be fed.

YOUR THOUGHTS

LABOR OF THE SOUL

39 Her Kinsman

"And Naomi had a kinsman of her husband's, a mighty man of wealth, of the family of Elimelech; and his name was Boaz." Ruth 2:1 (KJV)

God always seeks our best. He'll make a way. Do not attempt to outthink God with your own wisdom. He parted the Red Sea in our lives, He satisfied our thirst in the wilderness of despair, and He feeds us in famine. At wits' end, He will carry you through. "They reel to and fro, and stagger like a drunken man, and are at their wits' end. Then they cry out to the Lord in their trouble, and He brings them out of their distresses" (Psalm 107:27–28).

The same was true with Naomi. She had a relative in Bethlehem on her husband's side of the family whose name was Boaz, which means "fleetness." The vision from heaven's horizon was clear. Chapter one, in Moab: Naomi's family was weak. Chapter two, in Bethlehem: Naomi's family was mighty. In Moab, Naomi's family was poor. In Bethlehem, Naomi's family was wealthy. In Moab, Naomi's family died. In Bethlehem, Naomi's family was alive. "Behold, I am the Lord, the God of all flesh. Is there anything too hard for Me?" (Jeremiah 32:27). The answer? No.

Man will lie down and rise again throughout his life. Every night sleep is a death, the doorway to a new day. We awake through the visitation of God to a new life to be lived. "The sun also rises, and the sun goes down, and hastens to the place where it arose" (Ecclesiastes 1:5). Throughout nature this pattern is seen.

Stop and look closely. You'll find God's cycle of life and death and life again in the world around us. The lovely sight and scent of the lily is short-lived. In the twilight of its day, when its internal seed begins to grow, death comes to the flower. It wilts, waning away so the life within itself might be. The cycles of the seasons are seen—spring, summer, fall, and winter—faithfully fulfilling their course.

The death of Naomi's husband and sons to the natural eye looked bleak, but to the eye of the Spirit it's a glad day. "Better to go to the house of mourning than to go to the house of feasting, for that is the end of all men; and the living will take it to heart" (Ecclesiastes 7:2). God will be swift to ensure His promise to His people. Naomi had a lively, mighty, and wealthy kinsman.

The significance of this relative is described in the law:

> If brothers dwell together, and one of them dies and has no son, the widow of the dead man shall not be married to a stranger outside the family; her husband's brother shall go in to her, take her as his wife, and perform the duty of a husband's brother to her. And it shall be that the firstborn son which she bears will succeed to the name of his dead brother, that his name may not be blotted out of Israel" (Deuteronomy 25:5–6).

If a man in Israel died without a living son, the nearest male relative had a duty to marry the wife of the dead brother. He was to bear children for his deceased brother.

This kinsman became a husband, father, protector, vindicator, and redeemer for a woman without sons and whose husband was dead. The firstborn son unto the kinsman redeemer was given the name of the deceased brother to ensure the family name would not be blotted out among Israel. This is the redemption process in Israel, a man brought back from the dead.

Christ Jesus is our kinsman redeemer. He became a husband to the widow, a father to the fatherless, a protector of the violated, and a vindicator of those who have been wronged. Christ alone brings back from the dead all who accept Him.

Pick of the Crop: Naomi's kinsman of Bethlehem was everything her husband and sons were not and would exceed the longing of her heart. Israel's kinsman, the carpenter's son, is everything the nation wanted but could not see. The kinsman is waiting for those lost in their way to turn to Him. If you seek for God with your whole heart, you will find Him.

40 Desire to Serve

"So Ruth the Moabitess said to Naomi, 'Please let me go to the field, and glean heads of grain after him in whose sight I may find favor.' And she said to her, 'Go, my daughter.'" Ruth 2:2

Ruth had been feeding on Bethlehem's bread. She was consumed with the knowledge of the coming Redeemer, and armed with this knowledge, His Word became a fire within her heart. She desired to go out into the field and begin to labor.

Evangelizing, sharing the good news of Jesus Christ, is done in the hope of gathering souls to Him. Ruth hoped to find favor, leading her to the perfect location to work.

The disciple of Christ ought to go into the field in like manner, "witnesses to Me in Jerusalem, and in all Judea and Samaria, and to the end of the earth" (Acts 1:8). We, His disciples, go out into the world, into our communities for weekly fellowship or a day at the park passing out gospel tracts. Our daily waking hours ought to be consumed with service for the Lord.

Who wouldn't willingly serve the One who has unselfishly delivered us from suppression, depression, and death? A heart with a desire to serve God is a byproduct of fellowship with Him, experiencing His love for souls.

Salvation and a desire to serve are gifts. "For by grace you have been saved through faith, and that not of yourselves; it is the gift of God, not of works, lest anyone should boast" (Ephesians 2:8–9).

A service call came to Mary Magdalene, Joanna, and Susanna, women who had been healed by Jesus of evil spirits and diverse diseases, now found faithfully ministering unto Him, serving Him out of their own personal possessions (Luke 8:1–3).

Serving Christ may not place you within His immediate circle like these women were, yet His Spirit is with you. There are other parts of His vineyard that need tending. A certain man who had been possessed with devils sought to serve Christ in the presence of Christ. Jesus, knowing best, sent the man back to his family and former community, healed to begin serving in his hometown (Luke 8:38–39). Christ equipped him with the tools of his newfound trade, a testimony of what God had done.

Peter's call to service came immediately after an unfruitful night's work. At first, the light of Christ revealed his sinful nature, and Peter sought to separate himself from God's love, but Christ sought Peter's service to His ministry. Laboring in the darkness of this world hides our sinful nature, "and men loved darkness rather than light, because their deeds were evil" (John 3:19). The light of Christ exposes sin, and we must respond one way or another. Peter was delivered from his works of darkness that day, forsaking all to serve Christ (Luke 5:1–11).

When we are born again, our soul's desire is to see this miracle of God reproduced in the hearts and lives of others, bearing fruits of righteousness. Ruth saw those fields were ripe, ready for the harvest, just as our Lord said to His disciples, "The harvest truly is plentiful, but the laborers are few. Therefore pray the Lord of the harvest to send out laborers into His harvest" (Matthew 9:37–38).

This world—past, present, or pending—will never know a greater profession to be employed in than laboring for the Lord of the harvest. The world mocks, scoffs, and cries out against the Lord's hires. Some were stoned; others were imprisoned and killed, "of whom the world was not worthy" (Hebrews 11:38). Yet a woman of Moab, a stranger, sought opportunity to glean.

Ruth has grown in her faith, actively demonstrating new-found knowledge of the law of God. She has an understanding of the Lord's provision for His poor widow. "When you reap your harvest in your field, and forget a sheaf in the field, you shall not go back to get it; it shall be for the stranger, the fatherless, and the widow, that the Lord your God may bless you in all the work of your hands" (Deuteronomy 24:19). The harvest is to bless both rich and poor. This blessing is twofold, to the Hebrew and to the Gentile, the stranger.

Pick of the Crop: Serving Christ is a lifelong labor of love. Retirement comes at death. Until then we're to "do business till I come" (Luke 19:13). Our service is not part time, rather a full-time practice beginning within our homes and branching out into the lost world. Serve as if your life depends on it. It most certainly does.

41 FAITH OF GLEANING

"Then she left and went and gleaned in the field after the reapers. And she happened to come to the part of the field belonging to Boaz, who was of the family of Elimelech." Ruth 2:3

It was early morning, the sweet smell of spring was in the air. Ruth headed out beyond the walls to the fields and rolling hills that surrounded the city. Bethlehem sat as a dazzling gem in a bezel setting. The sunrise was glorious, flashing rays of stammering light through the foliage. Bethlehem was a beauty: "Thy plants are an orchard of pomegranates, with pleasant fruits; camphire, with spikenard, spikenard and saffron; calamus and cinnamon, with all trees of frankincense; myrrh and aloes, with all the chief spices" (Song of Solomon 4:13–14 KJV).

Every breeze was like the breath of God. The morning dew was the sweat of His brow. The song of the sparrows echoed His praise. What a contrast to the land where Ruth used to dwell.

A bountiful season was on the horizon. The fields were white, ready for the harvest. Ruth lifted up her eyes to behold a certain man. She saw he was in authority over the reapers that had gathered in the field. Ruth neither looked nor sounded like the other women that had convened, yet she approached the man to ask his favor to glean in the field.

In Bethlehem, Ruth learned to communicate with the Hebrews. Living within the culture of Christ, away from the world, we too learn how to communicate with the family of God from a pure and sincere heart.

The man in charge of the reapers discovered Ruth was the Moabite woman who returned with Naomi. With the news of Naomi's companionship and Ruth's eagerness to work, she was granted employment.

God was quietly working behind the scenes to perform His Word (Jeremiah 1:12). We are beginning to see that link between God and humanity. Each person born in this world is woven into the plan of God and adds to His beautiful, global tapestry. God shows no favoritism (Acts 10:34). No matter who you are, in God's eyes your status can go from harlot to hero, pimp to priest, by His grace.

You can't arrive unless you go. The Lord requires active participants in His ministry. Ruth went and worked as a gleaner in the field. She demonstrated her faith in God by her willingness to work. "But someone will say, 'You have faith, and I have works.' Show me your faith without your works, and I will show you my faith by my works" (James 2:18).

Pick of the Crop: Gleaning is a gift of God that can be difficult work. It is gathering spiritual truth to feed our hungry souls and the souls of others in this world. In the wilderness, Israel went out six days a week to gather the bread of heaven—manna (Exodus 16:14–30). So likewise is the gleaning of Boaz's field. Our spiritual sustenance comes from the daily gleaning of God's Word. Pray to God to give you a renewed taste for His Word.

42 The Need for Discipleship

". . . after the reapers." Ruth 2:3

Ruth followed after seasoned reapers who may have "borne the burden and the heat of the day" (Matthew 20:12). That is to say, the Jews were first to partake of the blessings of God and His long dealings with the people and the nation; afterward came the Gentile. These were reapers with experience, who knew the ways of the field.

Reaping is both a joyful and difficult task, with days of delights and discouragements, especially where tares have been sown. That's one of the reasons mentoring in ministry needs to be common. It is a following after the reapers, discipling the newborn in the Christian life. A good mentor will build valuable spiritual lessons on gleaned truths for the faithful who will be able to teach others (2 Timothy 2:2).

We should remain cautious when new believers are given a role to play in service to God. If their zeal is not channeled correctly, they will commit errors in the field. "As iron sharpens iron, so a man sharpens the countenance of his friend" (Proverbs 27:17). Fellowship in the labor of God helps believers in their development. Building godly friendships is another way of helping equip the workers for the ministry. It's hard to imagine Ruth overstepping the reapers in her zeal to serve. She would be out of place.

The twelve disciples of Jesus shadowed the Shepherd for three years and witnessed His glory at work, being taught how to deal with their faults and failures, truth and mercy, love and temperance. "And there are also many other things that Jesus did, which if they were written one by one, I suppose that even the world itself could not contain the books that would be written. Amen" (John 21:25).

The Lord told the disciples of John the Baptist, "Go and tell John the things you have seen and heard" (Luke 7:22). Through thick and thin, the disciple, as well as those being discipled, are there for one another. This is the way of discipleship.

"Paul chose Silas and departed, being commended by the brethren to the grace of God" (Acts 15:40). The two encouraged and strengthened each other in the ways of God. Ruth had the reapers and Naomi to instruct and encourage her.

Pick of the Crop: A disciple is someone who is learning the life of Christ. That disciple's love of Christ is greater than a love of family or self. The disciple of Christ has their own cross to bear and has counted the cost of their discipleship. (Luke 14:26–33). Don't forfeit the glory that is to be revealed for a false sense of discipleship where no cross is found. "Find one, teach one, be one" is the mantra for those being discipled in today's world.

43 GREATER THAN BOAZ

"Now behold, Boaz came from Bethlehem, and said to the reapers, 'The Lord be with you!' And they answered him, 'The Lord bless you!'" Ruth 2:4

Boaz came from Bethlehem as did Jesus. His mother was a Gentile who was satisfying the revolving door of the flesh when she heard the call of God. She longed for a new profession, and the Lord sent, as it were, reapers to harvest her. Rahab, the harlot of Jericho, married a Hebrew and gave birth to Boaz (Joshua 2:1–24, 6:22–23, Matthew 1:5).

> Many, O Lord my God, are Your wonderful works
> Which You have done;
> And Your thoughts toward us
> Cannot be recounted to You in order;
> If I would declare and speak of them,
> They are more than can be numbered. (Psalm 40:5)

"Now behold, Boaz." To all who occupy his field, take note. It's Boaz, whose name means "fleetness." His name precedes him. His wealth, his authority, his power, his compassion, his love—behold it's Boaz.

And there is someone greater than Boaz! "Indeed a greater than Jonah is here. . . . and indeed a greater than Solomon is here" (Matthew 12:41–42). "Behold! The Lamb of God." He surpasses Boaz in all his glory. Look upon Him; consider the wondrous works He has done. He "takes away the sins of the world!" (John 1:29).

"Behold my servant, whom I have chosen; my beloved, in whom my soul is well pleased: I will put my spirit upon him, and he shall shew judgment to the Gentiles" (Matthew 12:18 KJV).

"Behold, thy King cometh unto thee, meek, and sitting upon an ass, and a colt the foal of an ass" (Matthew 21:5 KJV). He is the prophesied Christ.

"Behold the man," the suffering Christ, bloodied and bruised for our sakes, donning the cursed crown (John 19:5). Look at Him. See His shame. Feel His pain. It is He who paid the price that we could not pay. He's the Great Redeemer.

"Behold your King," the suffering King who laid His glory down for you and for me (John 19:14).

"Behold the place where they laid him" (Mark 16:6 KJV). The Crucified has risen, conquering death.

"Behold, Jesus met them, saying, 'All hail.' And they came and held him by the feet, and worshipped him" (Matthew 28:9 KJV). The risen Redeemer is worshiped.

"Behold, I am alive for evermore, Amen; and have the keys of hell and of death" (Revelation 1:18 KJV). Christ conquered hell and death.

"Behold, I come quickly: hold that fast which thou hast, that no man take thy crown" (Revelation 3:11 KJV). Hold close to heart our faith in Him, our love for Him, our trust in Him to fulfill His promises toward us.

"Behold, I stand at the door, and knock: if any man hear my voice, and open the door, I will come in to him, and will sup with him, and he with me" (Revelation 3:20 KJV). The choice is yours whether to let him through the door of your heart or not.

"Behold, the Lion of the tribe of Judah, the Root of David, hath prevailed to open the book, and to loose the seven seals thereof" (Revelation 5:5 KJV). Jesus the man has done that which no other man will ever be able to do.

"Behold, I come as a thief. Blessed is he that watcheth, and keepeth his garments, lest he walk naked, and they see his shame" (Revelation 16:15 KJV). Walk worthy of the call of Christ.

"Behold, I come quickly; and my reward is with me, to give every man according as his work shall be" (Revelation 22:12 KJV). A reward from Heaven's Christ is awaiting all those who have overcome.

The very God and wholly man Jesus Christ, son of God— "behold, your God" (Isaiah 35:4).

No greater sight,
No greater sound,
No greater smell,
No greater touch,
No greater taste can mortal tell.

No greater man,
No greater friend,
No greater son,
No greater test,
No greater rest will there be sung.

No greater word,
No greater death,
No greater hope,
No greater peace,
No greater joy can men employ.

No greater love
No greater life will ever be,
The sacrifice of Jesus Christ, and now I'm free!

"The Lord be with you," Boaz said. O how we need the presence of the Lord of the harvest with us in the reaping process. There are too many reapers attempting this work without Him, employing worldly men with worldly methods in the hopes of spiritual bounty.

The reapers responded to Boaz with a cordial pleasantry of that day, "The Lord bless thee." How might our response be to all that God has and is doing within our hearts and lives today? Are we careful not to murmur over the manna He freely bestows? Do we readily proclaim blessings to God for who He is? Learn a lesson from His reapers, and bless the Lord.

Pick of the Crop: Consider how great this man is: He's our great King (Psalm 48:2) and a great light (Matthew 4:16). His jealousy is great for Jerusalem and Zion (Zechariah 1:14). He is great in goodness and beauty (Zechariah 9:17). He is abundant in mercy (Luke 1:58). His love is great toward His friends (John 15:13). He is our great salvation (Hebrews 2:3) and our great reward (Genesis 15:1).

44 Life's Labor

"Then Boaz said to his servant who was in charge of the reapers, 'Whose young woman is this?'

"So the servant who was in charge of the reapers answered and said, 'It is the young Moabite woman who came back with Naomi from the country of Moab. And she said, "Please let me glean and gather after the reapers among the sheaves." So she came and has continued from morning until now, though she rested a little in the house."' Ruth 2:5–7

O to learn the value of time over treasures! Without the former, the latter can't be utilized. Within Bethlehem, Ruth understood this truth and wasted no time finding employment.

This lesson can be learned by examining the life of a certain man who was rich in possessions and poor on time, shrewd with wealth, foolish with his future. He trusted in his treasures while misplacing valuable moments. He was pitifully poor with the time he possessed.

See how our Lord's earth was fruitful in her furnishing to the rich man, and yet, he was found meager toward his own soul.

> And he thought within himself, saying, "What shall I do, since I have no room to store my crops?" So he said, "I will do this: I will pull down my barns and build greater, and there I will store all my crops and my goods. And I will say to

> my soul, 'Soul, you have many goods laid up for many years; take your ease; eat, drink, and be merry.'" (Luke 12:17–19)

God will appraise every man a fool "who lays up treasure for himself, and is not rich toward God" (Luke 12:20–21).

This rich man's figures were faulty, equating increased earnings with increased years of life. If we would honestly ask God to direct our use of time on this earth, we'd begin to see time's scarcity, and the scarcity of a thing increases the value thereof. We would see ourselves as mortals in this world. We would learn that treasures on earth stored are not treasures in heaven retained. Earthly treasures are tarnishing.

"Do not labor for the food which perishes, but for the food which endures to everlasting life, which the Son of Man will give you, because God the Father has set His seal on Him" (John 6:27).

Ruth knew there was a set time to reap, and she valued that time, taking full advantage of the moment. The same holds true of you and me. God has given everyone a set time on this earth. "The number of his months is with You; You have appointed his limits, so that he cannot pass" (Job 14:5). Spend what time you have in wisdom serving Him. "So teach us to number our days, that we may gain a heart of wisdom" (Psalm 90:12).

Work is a good thing, and we're expected to provide for ourselves and our family. "If anyone will not work, neither shall he eat" (2 Thessalonians 3:10). This is the correct way. But many have been deceived with a false sense of satisfaction working for temporal treasures. Pursuing things that cannot satisfy is as futile as attempting to catch the wind in your hands, "and indeed all was vanity and grasping for the wind. There was no profit under the sun" (Ecclesiastes 2:11). Over and over again, man attempts to fill a spiritual void with tangible trinkets.

Working for Christ requires a change of focus, taking our eyes off passing pleasures of self-labor and working for Christ who has eternal rewards. Work at obeying His Word.

Pick of the Crop: Before coming to Christ, whatever it was that occupied your mental labors most was the labor of your life. Physically you may toll in the service of manufacturing, but if your mind is working to succeed in Christ by doing a work pleasing to Him, your labor is not in vain in the Lord. You may not be working in what the world labels as ministry, but if the spirit of ministry is working in you then that's your life's labor. There is coming a day when all will eat the fruit of their labors. May it be in Christ.

45 WORKING FOR CHRIST

Take this practical lesson into consideration. The Bible tells us not to covet. "You shall not covet your neighbor's house; you shall not covet your neighbor's wife, nor his male servant, nor his female servant, nor his ox, nor his donkey, nor anything that *is* your neighbor's" (Exodus 20:17). Do not indulge an inordinate craving for things of this world. How is this accomplished? By working at keeping your mind on obeying Christ. When a spirit of covetousness, which is lust, arises in your heart, refuse to entertain it. Don't give any mental energy toward it whatsoever. Resist it with the sword of the Spirit, which is the word of God (Ephesians 6:17). Until you do this, there is little chance of victory.

When you agree within your soul to obey Christ at all cost, you'll notice a battle has begun within you, a battle within your mind. You will have to cast down imaginations and high things that rage against God's revelation, "bringing every thought into captivity to the obedience of Christ" (2 Corinthians 10:5). This process takes work, mental labor moment by moment, day after day. Should the spirit of covetousness surface in your mind one hundred times a day, refuse to obey those thoughts each time.

Is doubt diminishing your day? Is fear threatening your peace? These are darts from the wicked one, our adversary, and he's warring for your soul. God's answer to this wicked onslaught is the shield of faith—"able to quench all the fiery darts of the wicked one" (Ephesians 6:16).

Faith's shield has to be exercised, tried, and tested. How else will we learn to rely on it? It's a spiritual tool, a gift of God for the spiritual battle we're in. Faith takes work. Picture a warring soldier defending the fortress of his or her heart. The shield is held firmly by trusting in the one who provides. This shield is in a steady, controlled, continuous rotation around the warrior, guarding whichever side a suspected dart may approach. The more we learn to work with the shield of faith, the bolder we become. Notice, when the next volley of darts are released, we will be able to sense them approaching by the Spirit of God. Sin is never swifter than God's Spirit.

We're co-laborers with Christ. Ruth understood she was to begin to work in her newfound status in Bethlehem. Where God places, God provides.

Pick of the Crop: The followers of Christ are literally employed by Him. He's never late in rewarding His workers for their labors, and as employees we should put our best foot forward. But there are many who are consistently late in their quiet time with Him or in obeying a special task He has requested. Working for Christ is working with Christ and not for our own pleasures. Ask God to give you a diligent heart to serve with promptness in every area of your labors.

46 In Boaz's Field

"Whose young woman is this?" Ruth 2:5

Boaz owned the land and the harvest. He employed the reapers. He knew them by name. Today a new employee caught his watchful eyes. Boaz's unnamed servant told him Ruth's testimony of returning with Naomi from Moab. The servant relayed Ruth's desire to glean and gather after the reapers among the sheaves. He told of her diligent service. She was a good and faithful servant.

Are we like-minded in our current employment, or do we give occasion for others to stumble?

Before salvation, those that are now called by Christ were the servants of sin with fruits unto death. "For when you were slaves of sin, you were free in regard to righteousness. What fruit did you have then in the things of which you are now ashamed? For the end of those things is death" (Romans 6:20–21). We labored feverishly for that tyrant taskmaster, reaping temporal rewards. We groped in the darkness of depravity, opposing ourselves. We were as this current age, "having their understanding darkened, being alienated from the life of God, because of the ignorance that is in them, because of the blindness of their heart" (Ephesians 4:18). "But God be thanked that though you were slaves of sin, yet you obeyed from the heart that form of doctrine to which you were delivered" (Romans 6:17).

Rejoice, for the Lord has found employment for us! Now let's serve Him with whole hearts and greater zeal than that of our former master. There are many areas of Boaz's field to labor in, his keeper is waiting to direct the next employee to the work at hand.

God is an equal-employment-opportunity God. His fields are open to all the nations and tongues of people on the earth. "Come ye near unto me, hear ye this; I have not spoken in secret from the beginning; from the time that it was, there am I: and now the Lord GOD, and his Spirit, hath sent me" (Isaiah 48:16 KJV). O that the lost would simply come and see. Christ has a place for you in His field. There's plenty of work to do in His name, and He will equip you with the gift needed to accomplish your call.

"So she came and has continued from morning until now, though she rested a little in the house" (Ruth 2:7). We are to continue in Christ, not wavering nor backsliding in the things that He has called us to do. Ruth fit right into her position, stopping briefly in the house for rest. Boaz had provided a period of refreshment from the rigors of reaping in his field. It was a necessity and should never be rebuked. We ought to pause throughout the day and lift up our hearts to the Lord and pray, giving thanks for what he has done. A contemplative, quiet time to ease our hearts and minds for the labors ahead.

He found me in Moab, beneath mulch and mire,
In a land brutal to man, my soul's need dire.

He called me from Moab, to seek planes much higher.
To the land of Bethlehem, in Boaz's field for hire.

He keeps me from Moab, with peace a blazing fire.
Beulah land at hand, in Christ I stand, my love and desire.

Pick of the Crop: Boaz's field was ripe for the harvest, open to whosoever will come and work the area. The field of our Lord is "already white to harvest" (John 4:35). He's calling for laborers, but you must be willing to accept the call. There are many areas within his vast field suited for you. Don't delay; come to Christ Jesus today.

47 LISTEN, MY DAUGHTER

"Then Boaz said to Ruth, 'You will listen, my daughter, will you not? Do not go to glean in another field, nor go from here, but stay close by my young women. Let your eyes be on the field which they reap, and go after them. Have I not commanded the young men not to touch you? And when you are thirsty, go to the vessels and drink from what the young men have drawn.'" Ruth 2:8–9

Boaz's first words to Ruth were very important. She would have to be willing to listen to his instructions. An unwillingness to follow the word of Boaz would be a sign of a rebellious heart similar to the heart of every man.

What more could God have done for the souls of this world? The heavens declare the glory of God, His prophets preach repentance, and His Word walked among us for a time. "But they refused to heed, shrugged their shoulders, and stopped their ears so that they could not hear" (Zechariah 7:11). Not so with Ruth. Boaz's every word would be hidden in her heart.

"Do not go to glean in another field, nor go from here." Boaz did what any good employer would do, instructing his new employee in what is expected. Don't leave here to go to another field. Stay close to my maidens. In other words, don't let the eyes of your desires wander.

Once the act of salvation has been secured, the will may continue to weave itself in and out of barley and chaff resembling the fields of Moab. "For the flesh lusts against the Spirit, and the Spirit against the flesh; and these are contrary to one another, so that you do not do the things that you wish" (Galatians 5:17). Boaz was a jealous employer, and God is a jealous God (Exodus 20:5). Don't give Boaz any reason to doubt your faithfulness to him.

"Stay close by my young women." Boaz had set others in fellowship with Ruth, leading the way she should follow. Other fields, gospels, or strange doctrines we have been warned not to enter into. Let your eyes be single, fixed on the field of Boaz. *Stay focused on the field where I've employed my maidens and there remain*—that was Boaz's desire for Ruth. "Have I not commanded the young men not to touch you?" Boaz had spoken a word of protection around Ruth. In him there was safety.

Pick of the Crop: The fool will despise wisdom. We are to be swift to hear and slow to speak (James 1:19). All the words of Christ are for our protection and profit. He doesn't make suggestions. There are many distractions in this world today in an attempt to drown out the Word of the Lord. If you're not listening to the Lord of the harvest, be assured you're listening to the world, your flesh, or the devil.

48 Do You Thirst for God?

"And when you are thirsty, go to the vessels and drink . . ." Ruth 2:9

There would come dry, parched times working in the field, and for those moments Boaz had made provisions. Go drink what he has provided. Notice it is water from Bethlehem's well.

Do you have a thirst for God? He's calling. "Ho! Everyone who thirsts, come to the waters" (Isaiah 55:1). In the natural world, nothing satisfies like water. The same holds true in the spiritual world with God. He alone satisfies the thirst of souls! "As the deer pants for the water brooks, so pants my soul for You, O God" (Psalm 42:1). "I opened my mouth and panted, for I longed for Your commandments" (Psalm 119:131).

David would one day cry out in the midst of the battle, "Oh, that someone would give me a drink of the water from the well of Bethlehem, which is by the gate!" (2 Samuel 23:15). Bethlehem's well speaks to us of Jesus Christ. He has an endless supply of spiritual water to satisfy the thirsting soul.

Unknown to David, three of his mighty men risked their lives to bring Bethlehem's water to their king. After recognizing the significance of their love for him and the great value of their sacrifice, David pours out the water unto the Lord as an offering (2 Samuel 23:13–17).

The Well of Bethlehem, Jesus Christ, our King in battle, would make David's gesture His passion. "Because He poured out His soul unto death, and He was numbered with the transgressors, and He bore the sin of many, and made intercession for the transgressors" (Isaiah 53:12).

Ruth had been invited to freely drink from the water of Bethlehem, and so have we. Do you thirst for peace within your heart in a dysfunctional world? Then the Well of Bethlehem's your choice. Drink freely and satisfy your soul's thirst.

Recall another woman, a stranger who met Jesus by a well. The topic of thirst spilled over, and as others before, she desired water from the well He distinctly described. As with Ruth, she was instructed on the terms of employment. True service would be done in spirit and in truth. She accepted His offer and immediately began laboring in her city, reaping fruits of the harvest (John 4:4–42).

He asked a drink from me, emptied at noonday,
I sensed He was a prophet from land far away.
I said, "Messiah's coming! Proclaiming, all will see."
He said, "Seek no further. Behold I am He."
He asked a drink of me, thirsting for my soul,
Wearied by His journey through heaven to earth His toll.
He met me by a well, alone I had no friend.
I drank His living water and never thirst again.

"For we are labourers together with God: ye are God's husbandry, ye are God's building" (1 Corinthians 3:9 KJV).

Pick of the Crop: Your soul's satisfaction is found in working for God. The desire of your heart is found in Him. The yearning of your spirit can never be quenched drinking from the cesspool of this world. He alone satisfies the thirsty soul (Psalm 107:9).

49 Bowing in Wonder

"So she fell on her face, bowed down to the ground, and said to him, 'Why have I found favor in your eyes, that you should take notice of me, since I *am* a foreigner?'" Ruth 2:10

Ruth bowed before Boaz. All humanity will bow before Jesus (Romans 14:11). Note closely the way we should respond to the Lord of the harvest, with sincere gratitude, our hearts bowed before Him. Ruth was completely lost in the wonder of Boaz's grace toward her, a stranger. She couldn't fathom it, and neither can we.

After receiving word that David desired a wife, Abigail (whose name means "a father's joy") bowed her face to the earth in amazement of the man who requested her hand in marriage (1 Samuel 25:41). Her former husband had died. He lived a life labeled a fool (1 Samuel 25:25). Her husband to be, David, would be called a lover of God. Friends, when we trust in the God of mercies the unimaginable will occur, leaving you completely amazed. Both Ruth's and Abigail's husbands died and both would marry again to men who will exemplify the love of God, which ushered them to awe and wonder.

There were times in David's life when he thought on the wonders of God and asked, "What is man that You are mindful of him, and the son of man that You visit him?" (Psalm 8:4). Read again the words of David's heart as he was awestruck with amazement over God's knowledge of him and his people.

> But who am I, and what is my people, that we should be able to offer so willingly after this sort? For all things come of thee, and of thine own have we given thee.
>
> For we are strangers before thee, and sojourners, as were all our fathers: our days on the earth are as a shadow, and there is none abiding. (1 Chronicles 29:14–15 KJV)

The wonder of God dealing with humanity isn't restricted to this present age. On the contrary, the angels desire to look into the relationship between God and man (1 Peter 1:12). Unless there's an understanding of the sacrifice of God, there's little hope for looking into the depth of His love.

I asked God for strength, He gave weakness;
for help, I found affliction.
I requested alms, He took away.
Yet in the process of time,
I saw His wonderful strength in my weakness,
His love in my affliction,
and in my loss I gained Him.

Pick of the Crop: "Many, O LORD my God, *are* thy wonderful works *which* thou hast done, and thy thoughts *which are* to us-ward: they cannot be reckoned up in order unto thee: *if* I would declare and speak *of them*, they are more than can be numbered" (Psalm 40:5 KJV).

YOUR THOUGHTS

50 He is Fully Aware

"And Boaz answered and said to her, 'It has been fully reported to me, all that you have done for your mother-in-law since the death of your husband, and how you have left your father and your mother and the land of your birth, and have come to a people whom you did not know before.'" Ruth 2:11

Boaz was aware of Elimelech's departure from Bethlehem. He knew of his death in Moab, how Naomi and Ruth met, the marriages, the poor health of Naomi's sons, and their death. Boaz knew of Ruth's journey through the wilderness and her Jordan crossing. He knew of her entering into the Promised Land. Boaz was clearly aware of Ruth's love for Naomi, her people, and her God.

Boaz was fully aware of all that Ruth had done to reach Bethlehem and his field. Likewise, our inner sacrifices are clearly manifested outwardly. Leaving father, mother, and land of birth for another way of life will not go unnoticed. Our sacrifices, minimal or monumental, are all seen. "And there is no creature hidden from His sight, but all things are naked and open to the eyes of Him to whom we must give account" (Hebrews 4:13).

God knows our inner thoughts. We're all exposed before Him. Ruth agreed in her heart to change her way of life, a decision hidden before men, seen of God. Her inner life of the heart would be made manifest outwardly. Boaz had begun to reveal the heart of Ruth.

Another lovely story is told of a woman who for twelve years had an ailment which burdened her. She spent all that she had on the physicians of that day, suffering tremendously at their hands, and her condition grew worse. One day she heard about Jesus and said, “If only I may touch His garment, I shall be made well” (Matthew 9:21). The Messiah mended the woman from within and revealed her openly to all. Jesus knows all that has occurred within our lives to get us to where we are in Him. So too, God mended Ruth’s sinful, stricken heart and began to open her up to those in Bethlehem.

Pick of the Crop: The eyes of the Lord are throughout all the earth. He is the Lord that sees. All other gods are the works of men’s hands. They have eyes but they see not, ears but they hear not (Psalm 115:5–6). Our God knows the decisions of our hearts, our pains and pleasures, longings and loving. All our sacrifices are witnessed and weighed by Him.

51 And He Will Reward You

"The Lord repay your work, and a full reward be given you by the Lord God of Israel, under whose wings you have come for refuge." Ruth 2:12

Boaz emboldened Ruth with the encouragement that her trust in the Lord God of Israel will not go unrewarded. Dear saints, have you sought shelter and protection from the storms of life under the wings of God? Rejoice! He's both a refuge and a reward.

Jesus told those who followed him, "Everyone who has left houses or brothers or sisters or father or mother or wife or children or lands, for My name's sake, shall receive a hundredfold, and inherit eternal life" (Matthew 19:29). Everlasting life is found in God.

It's also important to receive encouragement in our labors. Encouragement is found in fellowship and in the Word of God. Meditate for a moment on the following scriptures.

> Your righteousness *is* like the great mountains;
> Your judgments *are* a great deep;
> O Lord, You preserve man and beast.
> How precious *is* Your lovingkindness, O God!
> Therefore the children of men put their trust
> under the shadow of Your wings.
> They are abundantly satisfied with the fullness
> of Your house,
> And You give them drink from the river of Your pleasures.

For with You *is* the fountain of life;
In Your light we see light. (Psalm 36:6–9)

My mouth shall tell of Your righteousness
And Your salvation all the day,
For I do not know *their* limits.
I will go in the strength of the Lord GOD;
I will make mention of Your righteousness, of Yours only.
(Psalm 71:15–16)

O Lord, You have searched me and known me.
You know my sitting down and my rising up;
You understand my thought afar off.
You comprehend my path and my lying down,
And are acquainted with all my ways.
For there is not a word on my tongue,
But behold, O Lord, You know it altogether.
You have hedged me behind and before,
And laid Your hand upon me.
Such knowledge is too wonderful for me;
It is high, I cannot attain it. (Psalm 139:1–6)

God has provided His complete counsel for success in this life whereby those who trust in Him will succeed. The words of Boaz have strengthened Ruth's heart, giving her peace of mind.

Pick of the Crop: The diligent who seek to serve the King are rewarded. The size of the prize doesn't matter when apprehending the giver of the gift is the goal. God is our exceedingly great reward (Genesis 15:1).

52 He Will Comfort You

> **"Then she said, 'Let me find favor in your sight, my lord; for you have comforted me, and have spoken kindly to your maidservant, though I am not like one of your maidservants.'" Ruth 2:13**

There is amazing comfort from the Almighty when we come to Him. This godly comfort was demonstrated through Boaz. It was unrealistic to think Ruth had completely severed her love for father and mother, even though her love of God was greater. Nevertheless, questions would have surfaced in regards to her family back in Moab. Are they well? Are any sick? Are her parents yet alive? Ruth had many unanswered questions, questions that had the potential to immerse her imagination in torrents of unrelenting torment. But Ruth found comfort in the friendly words of Boaz.

The Lord God has come "to comfort all who mourn" (Isaiah 61:2). We need comfort in difficult times, and God's comfort is found in His Word. When we accepted Christ, we rejected the world, and in doing so, we opened ourselves up for testing, trials, and affliction designed to draw us closer to Him, purifying us in the process.

> Remember the word to Your servant,
> Upon which You have caused me to hope.
> This *is* my comfort in my affliction,
> For Your word has given me life.
> The proud have me in great derision,
> *Yet* I do not turn aside from Your law.

> I remembered Your judgments of old, O Lord,
> And have comforted myself. (Psalm 119:49–52)

Friend or foe, at one time or another, disappointed us. Good intentions went bad or bad intentions intensified. The account of Job tells of his loss of health, wealth, possessions, children, wife, position, respect, distant family, neighbors, and friends. His wife failed him. The three friends who came to help him through his difficult time failed him. Finally Job cried out, "Miserable comforters are you all!" (Job 16:2).

Unless we've been comforted by God, we aren't equipped to extend the comforts of God to others. God is the God of all comfort, "who comforts us in all our tribulation, that we may be able to comfort those who are in any trouble, with the comfort with which we ourselves are comforted by God" (2 Corinthians 1:4).

The Scriptures are for our profit. "For whatever things were written before were written for our learning, that we through the patience and comfort of the Scriptures might have hope" (Romans 15:4). Boaz could effectively comfort Ruth because he himself received comfort from God. We ourselves can receive the comforts of God and release the comfort of God into the hearts and lives of all those who need comforting by the Spirit of God.

Pick of the Crop: "Comfort ye, comfort ye my people, saith your God" (Isaiah 40:1 KJV). For the people of God, there's comfort found in Him. His comfort is never late and is sufficient for where He sends it. Whatever your current state of difficulty, know this: God's comfort will greet you. "In the multitude of my anxieties within me, Your comforts delight my soul" (Psalm 94:19).

53 Unlike Your Maidservants

"I am not like one of your maidservants." Ruth 2:13

Ruth wasn't born a Hebrew. She was born a Moabite, worshiping the gods of Moab. True, she was not like the maidservants of Boaz. She was a poor widow of Moab, an outsider who didn't grow up under the laws of Moses. "For the law was given through Moses, but grace and truth came through Jesus Christ" (John 1:17).

Behold the wonders of God. With Ruth's past and present circumstances, she was the perfect person to receive God's future work. He loved Ruth and wanted His people and the world to know of His unsearchable love for the most marginalized person.

How can it be?
His love and favor extends towards me!

Ruth had seen much, endured much, traveled far, and then she found herself at the receiving end of God's grace. Gentiles rejoice! Those who pledge allegiance to God the Father, He accepts you. "For if you were cut out of the olive tree which is wild by nature, and were grafted contrary to nature into a cultivated olive tree, how much more will these, who are natural branches, be grafted into their own olive tree?" (Romans 11:24).

We are part of God's eternal plan. We've been grafted or adopted into the family of Yahweh. God is high above the laws of this natural world, taking that which is contrary in nature and creating life and unity. Ruth—wild, dead, and unfruitful in this world—had been grafted into God's vine along with the natural branches, the Jewish nation.

Pick of the Crop: God's eternal plan has been revealed to the Gentiles, a church unlike the maidens of the Lord of the harvest. By God's grace, Gentiles have been grafted in, becoming one with the nation of Israel. There's no partiality in the love of God for our souls. The Moabitess and the maidens are different, but they are one in Him.

54 Eat This Bread

"Now Boaz said to her at mealtime, 'Come here, and eat of the bread, and dip your piece of bread in the vinegar.' So she sat beside the reapers, and he passed parched grain to her; and she ate and was satisfied, and kept some back." Ruth 2:14

Boaz invited Ruth to mealtime, a time when all gathered to commune in fellowship. This is a time to discuss the day's events, family, harvest, land, and God. Boaz instructed Ruth to eat the bread. Their meal looked forward to the life of Christ, and today's communion reflects back on the life of Christ.

"And as they were eating, Jesus took bread, blessed and broke it, and gave it to the disciples and said, 'Take, eat; this is My body'" (Matthew 26:26). Christ is the Word of God, and the Scriptures are for our consumption to be studied daily, meditated on, and talked about. "Give us this day our daily bread" (Matthew 6:11). Our daily bread is given from The Bread of Life Christ Jesus. He nourishes the famished soul with something the world cannot offer.

"Dip your piece of bread." Your piece of broken bread in the communion meal is Christ's broken body. "And when He had given thanks, He broke it and said, 'Take, eat; this is My body which is broken for you; do this in remembrance of Me'" (1 Corinthians 11:24). That's your portion, your experience, your testimony in Christ, specific for you.

Take all that you know of Christ thus far in your life, and take the plunge. Go deeper into His love for you by dipping your piece of bread into the "vinegar" which points to the cup of His bitter sufferings and death. The taste of vinegar is not hidden. Its odor is second only to its pungent taste. Of the seven times the word *vinegar* is used in the New Testament, it surrounds the bitter suffering of Christ's crucifixion (Matthew 27:34 & 48, Mark 15:36, Luke 23:36, John 19:29–30 KJV).

Oh, how Christ wanted His disciples to experience His sorrows and anguish of heart in the garden of Gethsemane!

"What! Could you not watch with Me one hour?" (Matthew 26:36–40). What has Christ asked of you or me in the hopes of dipping us deeper into His sufferings for the love of souls?

Paul the apostle longed to know the fellowship of Christ's sufferings, "that I may know Him and the power of His resurrection, and the fellowship of His sufferings, being conformed to His death" (Philippians 3:10). And Ruth was tasting that which her soul had already consumed.

Pick of the Crop: Boaz encouraged Ruth to eat the bread he had provided, and our Lord has given Himself for the nourishment of the souls. Every word out of His mouth is life. The Bread of Life has offered Himself to those who hunger. Come, my friend, partake of His bread. Why seek nutrition from things that cannot satisfy?

55 SITTING BESIDE THE REAPERS

"So she sat beside the reapers . . ." Notice the place where Ruth was seated, not relegated to distant association. She was one with the reapers, side by side in communion and fellowship.

Jesus complemented this thought in the New Testament, telling the story of a householder who hired laborers to work in his vineyard early in the day for an agreed amount (Matthew 20:1-12). Throughout the day more laborers were hired for an agreed amount. Finally, at the eleventh hour a final group of laborers were hired for the same wages as those hired at the beginning of the day. The laborers hired at the beginning of the day began to think they would receive more wages than the others, but they did not. All received the same wage. The men hired at the beginning of the day said to the lord of the vineyard, "These last men have worked only one hour, and you made them equal to us" (Matthew 20:12). The same was seen in the life of Ruth when she was placed side by side with Boaz's reapers.

Think back to a time when the Lord caused you to cross paths with a truly mature brother or sister in Christ. Remember how your heart burned with encouragement and excitement about your journey while they shared with you the more excellent way? Those individuals are the reapers, skilled laborers in the field of Boaz. Come alongside and learn from them. For this is your calling, even your sanctification.

"He passed parched grain to her . . ." Boaz reached out, extending his arm toward Ruth, giving her parched grain to eat, grain that had passed through the fire. God reached out, offering His Son to a lost world, for all who were willing to taste and see. The Crucified One had passed through the vehement love flame of God (Song of Solomon 8:6)—a love for humanity so intense it engulfed Him unto death and yet He lives a fruitful life. Ruth did not hesitate to partake of the gift from the hand of Boaz and neither should we refrain to accept what our Lord offers to us, both bitter and sweet.

Pick of the Crop: O how the love of God is longing to advance the obedient heart to a closer fellowship with Him and His faithful servants! Those who diligently glean find themselves seated beside the reapers in close proximity to the Lord of the harvest, receiving directly from His hands. Ask God to seat you next to the reapers during this time of harvest. In doing so, you'll gather a greater understanding of the Master and the ways of the field.

56 Returning to the Call

"She ate and was satisfied, and kept some back." The blessings from Boaz's table overflowed so much that Ruth is unable to take it all in. She "kept some back," holding it close for future nourishment.

There are many things offered from the Father's table that we aren't able to consume at the moment. We shouldn't forsake them but simply hold them back and meditate on them. You'll find yourself consuming them, or even sharing them, later in life as your hunger grows.

Ruth willingly ate that which was sufficient for her and returned to her calling. She was not idle but active in her call to duty. Ruth recognized that a meal of rest and refreshment was for revitalization and not meant for permanent dwelling.

It's here where many of the called stop short in their labor for Christ, thinking the high calling could be apprehended prior to completing the harvest. Many of Jesus's followers, disciples other than the twelve, turned away from following Him prior to completing their course. "From that time many of His disciples went back and walked with Him no more" (John 6:66).

After the death and resurrection of our Lord, Peter and a few of the other disciples were found fishing and it was not for the souls of men, a profession of the highest honor, something Christ said they would do (John 21; Mark 1:17). Jesus appeared unto them, and through His admonishing of Peter to feed His sheep, Christ redirected His disciples back to their call.

A Shulamite woman, not fully understanding the way of the lover of her soul (which is a picture of Christ), was likewise admonished to feed the flock (Song of Solomon 1:8).

Returning to the call is not returning to your former way of life. It's the high call in Christ Jesus. We are laboring for the Lord of the harvest, ministering, touching, and reaching the lost souls in this world with the gospel of Christ.

Demas, a companion in the ministry with the Apostle Paul, forsook Paul, choosing to cut short his ministry because he loved the things of this world rather than the things of God: "for Demas has forsaken me, having loved this present world" (2 Timothy 4:10). You'd be hard-pressed to find a double-minded spirit residing in the heart of Ruth.

Pick of the Crop: Don't stop short of your calling; we are to complete the course set before us (Hebrews 12:1). Your time and training in the things of our Lord should not be in vain. "Therefore do not cast away your confidence, which has great reward" (Hebrews 10:35). If you're not in the race, you'll never finish.

57 Prosperous Gleaning

"And when she rose up to glean, Boaz commanded his young men, saying, 'Let her glean even among the sheaves, and do not reproach her. Also let grain from the bundles fall purposely for her; leave it that she may glean, and do not rebuke her.'" Ruth 2:15–16

Boaz planned to reward Ruth's service over and above what was required, invoking the law of grace. Ruth's desire was to glean among the sheaves. The apprentice work in the field can be overwhelmingly slow, laboriously gathering what the reapers left. These times are used to test a soul's true love of service. Imagine time after time walking behind the reapers with unyielding fruit, and yet the work must continue.

Look over the field and see the reapers gathering and bundling sheaves. In the distance we see Ruth gathering smaller, almost insignificant, individual stocks, examining them for beard and kernel. Now take note. Ruth has been promoted. She's allowed to glean among the sheaves.

"Let grain from the bundles fall purposely for her." Boaz commanded the workers to let handfuls fall on purpose for Ruth to gather. These were larger treasures of encouragement for what remains of the day. Ruth simply took God at His Word in regards to the law of reaping and gleaning. In response to Ruth's obedience, God proved Himself faithful by opening up the heart of Boaz to pour out blessings for her.

The field was Boaz's to use of his good pleasure. Recall the last time the windows of heaven opened for you, allowing a purposefully directed blessing to fall into your lap? It is God's to give of His good pleasure.

With such rewards, there are those who would reproach those who are tireless in their service. For them, the word comes, "Touch not mine anointed, and do my prophets no harm" (1 Chronicles 16:22 KJV).

Pick of the Crop: God is faithful. He'll reward the path of the prospector. "For in him dwells all the fullness of the Godhead bodily" (Colossians 2:9). Give faithful service to God, and He will faithfully reward above all we could ever ask for or imagine.

58 Threshing the Grain

"So she gleaned in the field until evening, and beat out what she had gleaned, and it was about an ephah of barley." Ruth 2:17

All who labor in this world for our Lord will be given a just measure, an exact amount, "an ephah" of reward for the service of gleaning. The days are coming to an end, dear saints. "The night is coming when no one can work" (John 9:4). Our works will be "beat out"—threshed, thoroughly examined and separated—under the direction of God. Only the good seed for Christ will enter into the city, that is, His heavenly kingdom.

The threshing floor of God separates the tares (the wicked) from the true seed (the righteous) "First gather together the tares and bind them in bundles to burn them, but gather the wheat into my barn" (Matthew 13:30). Ruth separated grain from husk by threshing what she had gleaned.

Living life with Christ teaches us to daily review our labors, separating husks that are habits, deeds, and desires which attempt to hold on to our new life in Christ, hindering the work of God. The separation of grain from husk happens at the place of resistance, a hard rough surface that may cause difficulty.

Some days you'll find a heavy shroud of husk hovering over your desired plans to read your Bible, pray, go to church, fellowship, or sing praises to the Lord. There will be those hard days in our lives when we repeatedly have to tell the flesh (our former life lived) no to all its desires. No matter how rough your situation may be, nor the difficulty that may ensue, you must begin to separate yourself from the husk that hinders. The husk is not carried back into the city, which is your refuge. Difficult days are tallied here on earth for those who seek a heavenly home. Taking stock in the day's work can be difficult; separating the husk reveals seeds of life, which are to be shared with others.

Pick of the Crop: Separating your new way of life from your old habits is a difficult task, an impossibility without the work of the Spirit of Christ. We can break free from our former life through His threshing instruments, which is a painful necessity for reaping the fruits of righteousness.

59 THE BLESSING OF HER ELDERS

"Then she took it up and went into the city, and her mother-in-law saw what she had gleaned. So she brought out and gave to her what she had kept back after she had been satisfied." Ruth 2:18

Ruth began her day hopeful and ended it bountiful. A morning in deficit finished with surplus. Ruth went out empty and returned full. Naomi saw and received the fruits of Ruth's labors. She received life-giving seeds from her once-dead daughter-in-law.

Naomi could no longer work as when she was younger. It was up to Ruth to bear the burden for them both. Ruth might have joined with the younger women in the surrounding region, whose youthful passions followed after young men, but she would not. Ruth knew Naomi had a need, and she was called to serve Naomi in her latter days.

Recall the tender love David extended toward his eighty-year-old companion, Barzillai. While returning to Jerusalem after fleeing his son Absalom, David offered Barzillai sweet fellowship in Jerusalem under his care and a place to eat always at the king's table (2 Samuel 19:31–40). Barzillai graciously declined the offer, citing his age. David kissed and blessed him before sending him home. Do you see the resemblance? David's love and concern for his elder statesman was the same love and concern Ruth had for Naomi. O that more hearts of today's youth would labor to bless those seniors around them who may be in want or need. Ruth demonstrated true compassion for her mother-in-law by bearing and sharing with her the blessings she received. Naomi was in need, and God through Ruth met those needs.

We are never to despise the old. It is by the grace of God they have journeyed this far. When we look upon the aged, we're looking into our future, if we live as long. Be thoughtful how you respond to them, being patient, kind, and tenderhearted. In your future, there's someone who will lead you.

Pick of the Crop: Young people who show compassion on their elders will find undiscovered treasure there. Our elders have experienced the bumps in the way and can teach novices how to handle them. In your effort to bless, you will be blessed by the fruit of old age (Psalm 92:13–14). Ask God to make away where you can extend a helping hand to the senior saints in His flock. You'll find a good reward for your labors, something money can't buy.

60 LABORING CONTRARY TO THE CALL

"And her mother-in-law said to her, 'Where have you gleaned today? And where did you work? Blessed be the one who took notice of you.' So she told her mother-in-law with whom she had worked, and said, 'The man's name with whom I worked today is Boaz.'

Then Naomi said to her daughter-in-law, 'Blessed be he of the Lord, who has not forsaken His kindness to the living and the dead!' And Naomi said to her, 'This man is a relation of ours, one of our close relatives.' Ruth 2:19–20

"Where have you gleaned today?" This is a question the faithful ought to ask themselves at the close of each day. This vein of thought works as a cognitive compass, realigning the heart, soul, mind, and strength "toward the goal for the prize of the upward call of God in Christ Jesus" (Philippians 3:14). Can we answer the above question with honesty? Have we been laboring in the field of another, contrary to the call? Don't be deceived by those tall, golden stocks, "tossed to and fro and carried about with every wind of doctrine, by the trickery of men, in the cunning craftiness of deceitful plotting" (Ephesians 4:14). On close examination, you'll find a field littered with the tantalizing tares of this world, which are used to tickle the ears of those who reject the pure gospel of Christ.

Jesus said, "Not everyone who says to Me, 'Lord, Lord,' shall enter the kingdom of heaven, but he who does the will of My Father in heaven. Many will say to Me in that day, 'Lord, Lord, have we not prophesied in Your name, cast out demons in Your name, and done many wonders in Your name?' And then I will declare to them, 'I never knew you; depart from Me, you who practice lawlessness!'" (Matthew 7:21–23). Where have you been working today? Are you truly laboring for God by your words and actions at the place where you're employed, or are you occupying space?

A great and terrible day awaits those who have been deceived in thinking they're working in the service of Jesus Christ only to be found in gross error. The question remains, "Where have you gleaned today?"

Pick of the Crop: This world has deceived many into believing they are employed in the field of the Lord. They can be seen sowing the seeds of another gospel and reaping a crop that lacks in luster. They are the tares of this world and will not endure the flames of our God. Don't be found opposing the gospel of Christ. Your soul is at stake.

61 Hope Restored

"Blessed be he of the Lord, who has not forsaken His kindness to the living and the dead!" The Spirit of God moved to take knowledge of His creation while we were in rebellion against His Love. God is in need of nothing. He's the supreme giver. It's a wonder why He pauses to take notice of us. It appears Boaz wasn't enriched by employing a poverty-stricken Moabite widow. God was bringing them to His planned end and Naomi's heart closer to His Spirit.

"This man is a relation of ours." Naomi was silent during Ruth's labors in Boaz's field. She knew of Ruth's service but was blind to the common bond building among the trio, and then, at the mention of his name, "the veil is taken away" (2 Corinthians 3:16).

The apple of God's eye, Israel, is blind to the relationship between the current Gentile age and its labors for God. They are aware of the Gentiles' dealings in the world but are largely unaware of the relationship that's being built between their God and the Gentiles. The labor of Israel and God's Church will soon come into full view when the veil is taken away, and what a wonderful day that will be.

Naomi's heart had turned back to God. She testified to the presence of God all along. Contrary to a popular idea today, God has not left off His kindness to His people, the nation of Israel past nor present. "Can a woman forget her nursing child, and not have compassion on the son of her womb? Surely they may forget, yet I will not forget you. See, I have inscribed you on the palms of My hands; your walls are continually before Me" (Isaiah 49:15–16). "Remember these, O Jacob and Israel; for thou art my servant: I have formed thee; thou art my servant: O Israel, thou shalt not be forgotten of me" (Isaiah 44:21 KJV).

Naomi was delighted to discover Boaz's connection to the blessings of Ruth. She was beginning to see a ray of light in the evening time. A threefold cord had been woven that will not be broken.

Pick of the Crop: "Hope deferred makes the heart sick: but when the desire comes, it is a tree of life" (Proverbs 13:12). Hope was multiplied into Naomi's heart, and her desire was restored. The plans of Jehovah were coming into focus, allowing her to see past her losses. In the economy of God, one seed of hope sowed in the fields of doubt will yield a bounty of assurances.

62 NAOMI'S WISDOM

"Ruth the Moabitess said, 'He also said to me, "You shall stay close by my young men until they have finished all my harvest."' And Naomi said to Ruth her daughter-in-law, 'It is good, my daughter, that you go out with his young women, and that people do not meet you in any other field.'" Ruth 2:21–22

Ruth testified to Boaz's harvest. Jesus is the Lord of the harvest (Matthew 9:38). The end of the harvest is drawing nigh. Where will you be found?

"Stay close by my young men . . ." Ruth was admonished to work close to the appointed young men for her safety. Boaz had instructed the young men not to lay hands on her.

"It is good, my daughter, that you go out with his young women." Naomi saw the wisdom of the plan. The men were for protection, the women for prudence. The latter was the more cautious approach, avoiding any appearance of sin.

Young women need to know the value and wisdom of senior saints in God. Older women can teach younger women in the way of holy living. Young ladies may feel their dress, friends, events, music, attitude, and lifestyle seem fashionable, but when viewed through the eyes of an older woman, their ways may require a godly reproach. Naomi was instructing Ruth how to conduct herself as a young woman concerning the things of God.

There's a lack of training young women in the world today. A course on modest conduct is needed. Examine the realm of dress. Lack of morals sometimes corresponds to a lack of dress. Many young women of this world march to the beat of "Less is Best" when it comes to dress. It has power over pliable male minds, a hook in the mouth of the lured. It's the way of the world, the methods of the flesh.

This conduct has made its way into the Tabernacle of God, and He's not pleased. No flesh will glory in His presence (1 Corinthians 1:29). A flesh fest is best left outside. Why give place to the devil? Older women, grandparents, and mothers, teach your daughters how to dress appropriately in and out of the church. "Do you not know that you are the temple of God and that the Spirit of God dwells in you? If anyone defiles the temple of God, God will destroy him. For the temple of God is holy, which temple you are" (1 Corinthians 3:16–17).

Pick of the Crop: The wisdom of a mother who desires God is lovely with gentle insights. No matter the difficulty of the situation, the wisdom of God shared in the spirit of love and meekness is required. The yoke of the youth comes in varying sizes and will lead them to plow in the field of another. But the wisdom of the godly, aged woman will aid in the removal of those shackles around the necks of the young.

63 Don't Go to Other Fields

Men, "the sword devours one as well as another" (2 Samuel 11:25). There's a lack of self-control in and out of the church of God. Men pride themselves on having physical strength and are quick to take on the challenges of mano-a-mano, while lacking the self-discipline to advance their spiritual faculties and strengthen their inner man. It takes spiritual strength from God to exercise daily.

Take the realm of wandering eyes. Men, it takes spiritual strength to control wandering eyes. "I have made a covenant with my eyes; why then should I look upon a young woman?" (Job 31:1). As the eyes wander so do the desires. Most men don't have the mental muscle to govern their eyes. If you fall to your eyes, you will fall to your desires. Men and women working in any ministry of God need to have a sense of the risk that awaits. And Naomi instructed Ruth on a more excellent way to walk.

"... and that people do not meet you in any other field." Again the warning goes out not to be found in someone else's field. Neither Boaz nor our Heavenly Father will ever be accused of failing to warn those they love. Don't be found grazing on teaching that's contrary to the gospel. Truth and substance are in short supply. The hireling over these fields doesn't care for your life. "But a hireling, he who is not the shepherd, one who does not own the sheep, sees the wolf coming and leaves the sheep and flees; and the wolf catches the sheep and scatters them. The hireling flees because he is a hireling and does not care about the sheep" (John 10:12–13).

Naomi's concerns were in conjunction with Boaz's. The same holds true in our lives. We don't need another gospel, nor the emerging methods of man's wisdom. "Let us hold fast the confession of our hope without wavering, for He who promised is faithful" (Hebrews 10:23).

"Draw near to God and He will draw near to you" (James 4:8). Flirting in the fields of another will keep you from growing close to God.

Pick of the Crop: There are many fields offering employment to the wandering souls of this world, fields that primarily satisfy the desires of the flesh. These fields grow false gods, false scriptures, false teachers, false saviors, false sanctification, which give a false hope of salvation. The hirelings over those fields do not have the love of God in their hearts, and your soul will work its way to hell if you labor there.

64 HARVEST TIME

"So she stayed close by the young women of Boaz, to glean until the end of barley harvest and wheat harvest; and she dwelt with her mother-in-law." Ruth 2:23

The Lord of the harvest has aligned you with people whom you should pursue closely for your edification. They may be father, mother, siblings, pastors, mentors, or role models—men and women with gifts and talents to help you in the way of the harvest. Ruth gleaned through two harvests, barley of the spring time and wheat in the summertime—two completely separate time periods with great overtones of a larger picture.

"And she dwelt with her mother-in-law." Ruth lived with her mother-in-law. This world has no small shortage of seniors, men and women well along in years, who have given up hope of ever retaining their youthful vigor. Now they desire simple friendships with the youth they once possessed, and there may lie opportunity for gleaning.

Naomi had returned to Bethlehem bitter, and now she was blessing and praising the Lord God. There was a change of heart. There were multiple areas of growth seen sprouting in and around Bethlehem's harvest, and Ruth delighted to be involved, choosing to stay and dwell with her mother-in-law.

It's harvest time, oh come with me,
Gather fruit for eternity.
The Master's calling, will you go?
Be ye filled. Gifts He'll bestow.

It's harvest time, the fields are white,
Let's gather and glean to Christ's delights.
The day far spent, laborers few,
Take heed to the Savior's calling of you.

It's harvest time, no more delay,
Accept your part; serve Him today!
Whosoever will let him come.
It's harvest time, souls to be won.

Pick of the Crop: This is the time of great celebration, a time of reaping what has been sown months before. Are you celebrating what you have sown into your soul and the souls of your family, friends, or neighbors? We all reap what we've sown (Galatians 6:7–8). Remember well: we reap more than what has been sown, and everything produces after its own kind. With this in mind, let's sow in righteousness and reap the rewards in the coming harvest.

YOUR THOUGHTS

REST OF THE SOUL

65 The Soul Rest

"Then Naomi her mother in law said unto her, 'My daughter, shall I not seek rest for thee, that it may be well with thee?'" Ruth 3:1 (KJV)

Neither prestige nor pleasures shrouded in flesh can ever cover a man's vast longing for rest within the soul. A healthy marriage is a place of rest from youthful passions. If left unbridled, these strong-felt feelings will pursue you throughout life, aiding in a restless, unrelenting search for temporal pleasures that will ultimately lead to the destruction of your soul.

How often we grow weary of mental strategies, vile in thought, with the hope of positioning ourselves for an encounter that will temporarily release worry, both psychologically and physically, only to have it return with greater injury. As the body rests at day's end, so too are we to learn the disciplines of rest within our minds, hearts, and souls.

Do you have sleepless nights? Are your thoughts confused throughout the normal course of the day? Worried over future events? That's the sign of an anxious heart. Dwelling upon the past? That's the sign of a depressed spirit. Come to Jesus for an alleviation of these ailments. You will find rest in Him.

A Shulamite woman in love, understanding the peace and contentment that comes with an inner rest, sought it vigorously, calling to her lover, "Tell me, O you whom I love, where you feed your flock, where you make it rest at noon. For why should I be as one who veils herself by the flocks of your companions?" (Song of Solomon 1:7). Realizing there were others who would attempt to divert her attention from the rest found solely in her lover, she sought diligently the instruction from his lips only.

David said, "Rest in the Lord and wait patiently for Him" (Psalm 37:7). Jesus called out to a weary, burdened world, "Come to Me, all you who labor and are heavy laden, and I will give you rest" (Matthew 11:28). There's rest in Jesus. He freely offers His rest to all who will simply come to Him.

In our former life of self-employment, we labored for that which perished, but (praise be to God) we have accepted the call to Bethlehem by faith and become employed in the field of Boaz. This also must be asserted: the sole block standing between a restful soul and a restless soul is unbelief. "Let us labour therefore to enter into that rest, lest any man fall after the same example of unbelief" (Hebrews 4:11 KJV). There's no rest found in unbelief. "But without faith it is impossible to please Him, for he who comes to God must believe that He is, and that He is a rewarder of those who diligently seek Him" (Hebrews 11:6). Your faith will assist you in the pursuit of rest. Unbelief prevented an entire generation from the rest found in God. "And to whom did He swear that they would not enter His rest, but to those who did not obey? So we see that they could not enter in because of unbelief" (Hebrews 3:18–19).

This rest isn't referring to salvation, since salvation cannot be obtained by works (Ephesians 2:8–9). This rest is rooted in the Branch of Jesse, Jesus Christ. Believing in Him and accepting His way of life is to refuse to obey the way of a sin-filled life. Resting in Christ's love prepares us for today and the life to come.

"Shall I not seek rest for thee, that it may be well with thee?" (Ruth 3:1 KJV). Naomi was a changed woman, her bitter spirit being threshed away. She had grown in faith. Her fellowship with Ruth was flourishing. New sprouts were seen. Now she delighted to seek rest for Ruth, rest only found in Boaz. She offered Ruth invaluable insight on how to achieve this rest. She knew where Boaz could be found and how to come before him. O for more godly, older women to come alongside the younger women to become "teachers of good things," helping them avoid the perils of passions (Titus 2:3).

Pick of the Crop: Man's attempt to work his way into favor with God through vain religious ceremonies is nothing more than the work of the flesh. Ruth had advanced with the favor of God and man. She was no longer laboring and would be found resting in the presence of Boaz. Christ has come to give complete rest to body, soul, and spirit. We may truly trust Him to deliver His rest in every situation with peace of mind.

66 Related to Christ

"Now Boaz, whose young women you were with, is he not our relative? In fact, he is winnowing barley tonight at the threshing floor. Therefore wash yourself and anoint yourself, put on your best garment and go down to the threshing floor; but do not make yourself known to the man until he has finished eating and drinking." Ruth 3:2–3

Naomi informed Ruth that Boaz was *our* relative. Can you see the works of God a little clearer now? Boaz was related to both a Hebrew and Gentile. Christ is akin to both Hebrew and Gentile.

The genealogy and kinsmanship was important to the Hebrews. Naomi was spot-on about Boaz being in their lineage. This was very important when it comes to the law of God and eternal rewards. Identifying Boaz as family opened up the possibility of their redemption, a redemption with great rewards.

Christ Jesus, our kinsman, in like manner had to have His lineage spot-on. God bore witness to it in two of the four Gospels, Matthew 1:1–17 and Luke 3:23–38.

Matthew's genealogy emphasizes our Lord Jesus Christ as the Son of David, attaching Him to the royal line of King David. Matthew's genealogy goes back to Abraham, father of the Jews.

Luke's genealogy emphasizes our Lord in His humanity, tracing Him back to Adam. Luke states Jesus was the son of Joseph, a common man.

Both genealogies identify Jesus as coming from the line of David, giving Christ, our kinsman, the legal title to Israel's throne.

When anyone comes to the liberating life of Christ, they are born into the family of heaven. The blood which Christ shed on His cross makes those who believe in Him a blood relative. It doesn't matter if you were born in Bethlehem or Moab; we're all family.

Heaven's Glory took on the likeness of humanity. "Inasmuch then as the children have partaken of flesh and blood, He Himself likewise shared in the same, that through death He might destroy him who had the power of death, that is, the devil" (Hebrews 2:14). "And the Word became flesh and dwelt among us, and we beheld His glory, the glory as of the only begotten of the Father, full of grace and truth" (John 1:14). Jesus Christ, the living eternal Word of God, became a man.

Christ took part of the same fiber of humanity in order to fully identify with us. "Therefore, in all things He had to be made like His brethren, that He might be a merciful and faithful High Priest in things pertaining to God, to make propitiation for the sins of the people" (Hebrews 2:17). Boaz identified with Elimelech's family needs and losses just as Christ identified with ours.

Pick of the Crop: We have been born again into the body of Christ, the family of God. His love for us is as vast as his love of Christ (John 17:23). Hallelujah, we've been made "heirs of God and joint-heirs with Christ" (Romans 8:17).

67 The Threshing Floor

"He is winnowing barley tonight at the threshing floor." Ruth 3:2

Boaz was industrious, wasting no time in the winnowing process, that is, separating true seed from chaff. All this took place on his threshing floor. The harvest was taken and thrashed out on the threshing floor, stroke after stroke, blow after blow. It was literally beaten. Threshing was nothing short of a violent process. Threshing separated wheat from chaff, seed from husk, men from boys, women from girls, heaven from hell, the godly from the ungodly, and God from gods.

The brevity of this life is coupled with varying degrees of thrashings and testing of our souls during diverse seasons of our growth. This is God's process of gleaning, reaping, and threshing valuable seed to share in the lives of others and for our own benefit. For our sakes, Christ was taken to God's appointed threshing floor and lifted up on His cross as an offering to God.

History teaches the Roman machine was very efficient with their pre-crucifixion brutality, and modesty was not in their mandate concerning malefactors. It's absurd to observe tradition's rendition of the crucified Christ hanging on His well-sculptured cross with His well-sculptured, minimally bruised body. To the contrary! "Surely he hath borne our griefs, and carried our sorrows: yet we did esteem him stricken, smitten of God, and afflicted. But he was wounded for our transgressions, he was bruised for our iniquities: the chastisement of our peace was upon him; and with his stripes we are healed" (Isaiah 53:4–5 KJV).

With a great degree of hate, both religious and Roman rulers abused Christ when His hour had fully come. From scalp to sole, Christ's flesh was literally torn, disfigured, mutilated, and desecrated. So severe was His threshing when nailed to the cross **naked**, He was not recognized as being a man. "So His visage was marred more than any man, and His form more than the sons of men" (Isaiah 52:14).

Christ's stripes were not feigned. His sufferings were not in vain. They were ordained from the God who reigns. We've been healed by Christ's stripes. His open wounds have healed our ill souls. "For consider Him who endured such hostility from sinners against Himself, lest you become weary and discouraged in your souls" (Hebrews 12:3):

- Christ was betrayed by His friend, Judas Iscariot (Matthew 26:47–50).
- Christ was falsely accused by the high priest, chief priests, elders, and the scribes, that is to say, the religious rulers/preachers of that day (Matthew 26:57–60).
- The educated, religious elite spat in the face of God and beat His Christ. (Matthew 26:67).
- Christ was denied by His disciple and friend, Peter (Matthew 26:69–75).
- Christ was mocked and beaten by Rome, the world power of the day (Matthew 27:27–31).
- Christ was crucified (Matthew 27:35).
- Christ died (John 19:30).
- Christ's side was pierced by a soldier's spear (John 19:34).

The alluring force that surrounds God's appointed threshing floor has been witnessed through the ages. Abraham built an altar with the intent to offer his son, Isaac, to the living God, a symbol of the sacrifice Christ Jesus would make (Genesis 22:1–14). Years later, David purchased that same threshing floor, built an altar and gave burnt offerings and peace offerings to God, pointing again to the sacrifice the God-Man, the Messiah, would make (2 Samuel 24:24–25). Solomon would build a glorious temple to the Lord God on that same threshing floor ground, symbolic of God's coming lamb, who would suffer among humanity and be sacrificed (2 Chronicles 3:1).

Is it nothing to you? Come and see.
Is there any sorrow like unto me?
The Lord has afflicted His anger out-poured.
Upon my soul the cost I bore.

Is it nothing to you that pass by
Beholding Christ suffer and die?
Forsaken of God. He asked why?
His life linked death's divide.

Is it nothing to you the victory seized?
He pardoned sins and answers pleas.
He rose from the grave, His love He gave.
It's solely Him with power to save.

The Winnower is very careful. "His winnowing fan is in his hand" (Matthew 3:12). It's judgment time. He's trying, testing, and threshing His harvest, ever so critical to examine His gatherings, releasing any flaw He may find. Tares have grown alongside His most valued seeds, cleverly mimicking the prize. But their time has come. "Let them be as chaff before the wind: and let the angel of the LORD chase them" (Psalm 35:5).

Pick of the Crop: Christ's threshing floor was designated in eternity past. His threshing pleased God (Isaiah 53:10), making us acceptable to the Father and staying the judgment. Mortal man can scarcely know the depth of the suffering of our Lord. David wrote of it (Psalm 22), the Apostles drank of it (Matthew 20:23), and Paul sought to know it (Philippians 3:10). The mutilation of His flesh birthed the mending of our souls.

68 Confession and Washing

"Wash yourself." Ruth 3:3

Man, with his own feeble attempts at religious piety, can never attain God or His holiness. Our parents in the garden needed Jehovah's covering for their transgressions. "Unto Adam also and to his wife did the LORD God make coats of skins, and clothed them" (Genesis 3:21 KJV). And we also need a covering.

Man's sin has separated him from God (Isaiah 59:2). "But we are all like an unclean thing, and all our righteousnesses are like filthy rags; we all fade as a leaf, and our iniquities, like the wind, have taken us away" (Isaiah 64:6). "At that time you were without Christ, being aliens from the commonwealth of Israel and strangers from the covenants of promise, having no hope and without God in the world" (Ephesians 2:12).

"But if we walk in the light as He is in the light, we have fellowship with one another, and the blood of Jesus Christ His Son cleanses us from all sin" (1 John 1:7). We're anointed by His Spirit (1 John 2:20), "for He has clothed me with the garments of salvation, He has covered me with the robe of righteousness" (Isaiah 61:10). The process of washing, anointing and covering is a welcome daily practice for the lover of God, sojourning in this perverse world.

Ruth washed herself in preparation to come into the presence of Boaz. The child of God in like manner ought to cleanse themselves from any defilement encountered throughout the day and approach God with a pure heart. "We know that we are of God, and the whole world lies under the sway of the wicked one" (1 John 5:19). Living in this wicked world, we're gathering dirt that so easily defiles; all the while God is encouraging His people to persevere. "Therefore, having these promises, beloved, let us cleanse ourselves from all filthiness of the flesh and spirit, perfecting holiness in the fear of God" (2 Corinthians 7:1). Washing and cleansing comes by the confession of our sins (1 John 1:9). Present yourself before the living God, and accept His steps of confession of sin for your cleansing benefit.

Those close to us may notice our need to be cleansed. If this message isn't relayed in the spirit of gentleness, meekness with love, we might resent their observation. Naomi saw a need in Ruth and gently instructed her daughter-in-law on the cleansing way.

Pick of the Crop: The priests of God washed themselves before coming into His presence (Exodus 30:17–21). We are expected to do the same. "Now ye are clean through the word which I have spoken unto you" (John 15:3). Confess your sins and turn to His Word for a cleansing of your soul.

69 Holiness, Not Happiness

"Put on your best garment." Ruth 3:3

We find, as Ruth did, man's modest means of covering ourselves in our "best garment" after a self-imposed cleansing is not sufficient to earn acceptance with God. God has His covering for us, and Boaz had his covering for Ruth.

God is holy, pure in character, unspotted by sin, perfect in wisdom and power. "No one is holy like the Lord" (1 Samuel 2:2). The angels around God's throne call out, "Holy, holy, holy is the Lord of hosts" (Isaiah 6:3).

"Who is like You, O Lord, among the gods? Who is like You, glorious in holiness?" (Exodus 15:11).

The high priest in the temple wore a gold medallion on his head with an engraving that read, "HOLINESS TO THE LORD" (Exodus 28:36-38).

We are commanded to be holy for God is holy (1 Peter 1:16). We're to be pure in heart, unspotted by the world, set apart for the Masters use. Happiness found in this world cannot measure up to holiness found in God.

God's ways of purifying us differ according to our need. There are deeper cleanings with varying degrees of pain, anointing, and covering to be had throughout our journey. Every area of our lives must be cleansed. We're called to holiness, not happiness, in the pilgrim's way, and happiness without holiness is penniless.

What profit is happiness on Earth only to be cast into hell unholy? Happiness is a temporal pleasure supported by your next favorable experience. Happiness is a castle made of sand washed away by the tides of life and built again by its patrons. Happiness is a transient treasure seized by disappointment.

Pick of the Crop: A life of holiness doesn't depend on the conditions of the world around. Holiness stands alone when all others fail. Holiness is a rare find. What can be like it in this world? Holiness is like a chaste virgin. Holiness is like a polished jadeite among grit. Holiness is like the number one standing alone among the infinite affections in the world.

70 The Dark Night

"'Then it shall be, when he lies down, that you shall notice the place where he lies; and you shall go in, uncover his feet, and lie down; and he will tell you what you should do.'

And she said to her, 'All that you say to me I will do.'

So she went down to the threshing floor and did according to all that her mother-in-law instructed her."
Ruth 3:4–6

Ruth's teaching came from Naomi, who was quick to relay that the final word on the matter would come from Boaz himself. "He will tell you what you should do."

Instructions given, Ruth willingly obeyed. Had there been any hint of duplicity, Ruth would not have obliged. God desires His called to respond willingly to His voice without waver.

Ruth left Naomi, veiled. Outside the walls of Bethlehem at night, where a spirit of fear might seek opportunity to afflict her soul, she sought Boaz.

We should never let a spirit of fear prevent us from seeking a closer walk with Christ, our Boaz, especially when traveling through the night, the darkest times of our faith. The world doesn't notice a dark night of faith. Only God and the heavenly bodies in the night sky bore Ruth witness.

The same holds true with you and me. Believe God, my friend. He sees the trying of your faith in the night. Our darkest moments are not hid from Him. "The darkness and the light are both alike to You" (Psalm 139:12). Will you trust Christ to see you through?

Ruth approached the threshing floor of Boaz. It was an eerie moment for her, pressing through the thick darkness. Every step in the night was a leap of faith propelling her toward the lover of her soul. "Your word is a lamp to my feet and a light to my path" (Psalm 119:105). Have you experienced the dark uncertainties on your journey? What more can be said but to continue your walk?

Ruth had grown from faith to faith, strength to strength, and glory to glory. She had learned to take comfort in the familiar presence they bring. O to trust Him!

Ruth was learning to trust God's leading during the delightful sunny days and the depths of darkness. When we trust in the Word, we increase our faith, thereby hoping in the union of our heart's desire. Ruth's desire was to rest in Boaz, a desire not far off.

With Boaz's threshing floor in view, the journey was not complete. Ruth remained still. She couldn't risk being seen. Quiet times in Christ, when your soul is still and calm, are never a moment to attract attention to your journey in Him. There are many spirits in the dark that would quickly attempt to hinder the union between two lovers.

Finally, her eyes apprehended Boaz in the night, accompanying his every move while patiently waiting. Can you see the picture? Ruth was an eyewitness to Boaz's work on his threshing floor. The darkest night of Christ's life on this earth came at the height of day (Luke 23:44), while laboring on God's appointed threshing floor. O to see a clear picture of Christ's dark night!

Time spent beholding Jesus at a distance is not time wasted, if His closeness is what you seek. If you continue in the way, there will come a time when the closeness shared with Christ departs. It may or may not be of your doing; nevertheless, you should keep your eyes fixed on Him. This will be for your growth.

There came a time when Mary Magdalene, along with other women who were close to Christ, watched Him at a distance (Mark 15:40).

Peter came to a place in his walk where he followed Christ at a distance (Mark 14:54). This place is never comfortable, but we must endure it.

When the time of their separation was complete, they found a renewed intimacy with Him. "Now when He rose early on the first day of the week, He appeared first to Mary Magdalene, out of whom He had cast seven demons" (Mark 16:9). He appeared another time to Peter and built up his love for God instructing him to feed His sheep (John 21:14–19).

How many of us wouldn't give all that we have to look upon the incarnate Christ and to follow His every step on this earth? He is the Boaz of the New Testament. The eyes of humanity will behold no greater sight than that of Jesus. O to behold Him in all that we think or do in this life and feel His presence always.

Pick of the Crop: There will come dark moments in life when the only certain thing is your reliance on Christ, "for we walk by faith, not by sight" (2 Corinthians 5:7). An unction has led you out on a dark road in the night with the hopes of meeting the lover of your soul. This is the dark night of faith. You're being led along as a child whose hands are firmly secured by a parent or as the blind who trust in the comforts of a staff. Only Christ knows the way you take.

71 Notice and Remember Where He Lies

"Notice the place where he lies" (Ruth 3:4). Mary Magdalene, who sought a closer union with the Lord, saw where the lover of her soul was laid, and came bearing precious ointments (Mark 15:47, 16:1). Ruth would see where her lover was lying and would come anointed. Mary sought Christ in the night and left with the rising of the sun (John 20:1, Mark 16:2). Ruth would seek Boaz in the night and will leave in the morning.

Notice the place where Christ was laid in death. The giver of life gave His life "a ransom for all, to be testified in due time" (1 Timothy 2:6). The Son God gave and the price Christ paid purchased our peace, something always to be remembered. The greatest death ever was that of the man Christ Jesus. Is the remembrance of Christ's cold body alive in the warm thoughts of your heart?

Jesus woke from death and met Mary's needs (John 20:16–17). Boaz would wake from sleep to meet Ruth's needs. Mary took the good news of Jesus to her loved ones (John 20:18). Ruth would take the good news of Boaz to Naomi, her loved one.

Night or day, high times or low, Jesus is always available to meet the needs of His people. He demonstrated His power over death. Can your problem be too difficult for Him to overcome? Remember the place where Jesus was laid? It was at that place that He accomplished what no other man could. He died as a perfect, sinless, spotless, acceptable sacrifice to God and then rose again. His death and resurrection are the places to mark our victory!

Pick of the Crop: Have you given quality meditation to where Christ was laid? The faithful women took notice. Christ was laid in a tomb that was not His own, where never a man was laid (John 19:41), for never a man died a death like Christ. The inauguration of His death was fitting. He was poor in death and rich in resurrection power. With His death, he hewed a resting place in the stony heart of humanity and was resurrected in the hearts of His disciples. Can you see where He was laid? Take time out to remember Christ in His death and in sweet communion this day (1 Corinthians 11:24).

72 Abandoned in Faith

> **"And after Boaz had eaten and drunk, and his heart was cheerful, he went to lie down at the end of the heap of grain; and she came softly, uncovered his feet, and lay down." Ruth 3:7**

After Boaz labored through his winnowing, he was nourished. It was a joyful time. He lay at the end of the pile of grain. Ruth was waiting patiently. Softly like a gentle breeze, she moved across the threshing floor toward him, uncovered his feet, and lay down.

"The wind blows where it wishes, and you hear the sound of it, but cannot tell where it comes from and where it goes. So is everyone who is born of the Spirit" (John 3:8). Of all the women in Bethlehem, Ruth was least likely to be found at Boaz's feet. Or was she? "For man looks at the outward appearance, but the Lord looks at the heart" (1 Samuel 16:7).

In the world of Moab, Ruth began to have a trust in God. She started an internal exercising of her spirit over her emotions. She learned to look past the things she saw and had known. She would come to experience the invisible things are more real than the things she saw.

A word or a promise of God was sufficient to move Ruth out of her comfort zone to an area where she would intersect God and His faithful promises.

A trust in God is like a child who trusts in the word of a parent, never for a moment doubting the sufficiency of the one who would supply the need or in some cases a desire. "If a son asks for bread from any father among you, will he give him a stone? Or if he asks for a fish, will he give him a serpent instead of a fish? Or if he asks for an egg, will he offer him a scorpion?" (Luke 11:11–12).

Ruth was literally stretched out in faith before God and Boaz. How many of us have taken God at His Word? How many of us have truly abandoned ourselves and our will, stretching out in faith at the feet of God? His covering awaits you. You will not be found ashamed.

Ruth's journey in and around Bethlehem carried her from Boaz's field to his floor and now to his feet. It's a mystery and it's marvelous in our eyes. The Spirit of God in Boaz was bearing witness with the Spirit of God in Ruth.

Pick of the Crop: "Have faith in God" (Mark 11:22). Christ laid down His life, and we ought to lay our lives down for Him. One way this is evident is our willingness to utterly trust Him in all that we do. God is the only one with the power to grant you favor. Ruth approached Boaz, trusting to be united to him in marriage. Her friendship with Naomi could not fulfill her desire for that union, nor could Ruth trust in her abilities.

My dear friends, trusting in your abilities to pray cannot hasten your request before God. It is faith in God alone that will draw down His blessing.

73 Covered by Christ

"And it came to pass at midnight, that the man was afraid, and turned himself: and, behold, a woman lay at his feet. And he said, Who art thou? And she answered, I am Ruth thine handmaid: spread therefore thy skirt over thine handmaid; for thou art a near kinsman." Ruth 3:8–9 (KJV)

Boaz awoke and discovered a woman lying at his feet. Who was she and what was her intent?

"Spread therefore thy skirt over thine handmaid." It was Ruth, and she was asking him to spread his skirt over her. Boaz was a near kinsman, and Ruth needed a covering. She was asking Boaz to marry her, be her covering, her protection, her security. She was grateful for employment in his field among his maidens, but she sought a closer, richer, fuller walk with Boaz, found only in marriage. She confessed her heart's desire for a covering immensely different from the covering she put on earlier. Cover me with your covering was Ruth's request.

She had realized a multitude of her best garments could never cover what the hem of Boaz's garment could. Her modesty sought a covering different from her own, and so should we.

"But I want you to know that the head of every man is Christ, the head of woman is man, and the head of Christ is God" (1 Corinthians 11:3). The apostle Paul plows close to the corn in our age of equality. The world would have you believing equality of the sexes means we're all the same. But equality between male and female does not mean we're the same. It's elementary, and a child can distinguish the most basic differences. The diversities of boy and girl have been passed down from the beginning of time throughout the cultures of the world. There are differences physically, emotionally; even at the cellular levels the two are different. Notwithstanding, both male and female must come before God with a repentant heart seeking salvation.

There's equality in transgression, "for all have sinned and fall short of the glory of God" (Romans 3:23). There's equality in salvation. "Look to Me, and be saved, All you ends of the earth! For I am God, and there is no other" (Isaiah 45:22).

God's order of equality in this world is: Christ, the head of man; man, the head of woman; and God, the head of Christ. Don't let the world's teaching rob you of God's order of equality. Every man and woman are equal in the eyes of God, even as God has ordered them.

Men abandon a blessed, full life in Christ when they fail to come under God's authority. A godly man is a Christ-following, God-loving man. He will never be satisfied in marriage until he humbly submits to Christ as his head, looking to Christ for his complete satisfaction. Under the leading of Christ, men learn how to love their wives as Christ loves His church and gave Himself for it (Ephesians 5:25). Husbands learn to see their wives as a precious vessel of God to be cherished.

A woman will never be loved in marriage as God would have her to be until she comes under the order of a God-given husband who strives with his whole heart to obey Christ. The wife learns to love her husband as Christ would have it (Titus 2:4–5). She learns to love him for the affection of Christ in him, looking past his failures and faults. All the rest, security, and peace of mind God has for a woman is found in this order.

Rejecting God's divine order is rejecting God. Don't allow the stubborn, bitter, vile spirit of this world to remove you from the equality found only in God. Ruth welcomed the covering of Boaz in her life, and so we should welcome God's covering in whatever role we're called.

Is Christ your covering? This world is ripe with marriages and ministries, all clothed in fleshly garments. God's indictment of the flesh stands firm. "It is the Spirit who gives life; the flesh profits nothing"

(John 6:63). "For I know that in me (that is, in my flesh) nothing good dwells" (Romans 7:18).

"For the flesh lusts against the Spirit, and the Spirit against the flesh; and these are contrary to one another, so that you do not do the things that you wish" (Galatians 5:17).

Only the blood of Christ can cover our fleshly deeds. It's His blood, His righteousness, His sufferings, and His great victory past, present, and future that shield us from the world. Have you believed this for your soul? If so, you are now justified. Rejoice! Your justification is salvation without condemnation.

Pick of the Crop: Christ is our protector, our covering, and our shield. "He shall cover thee with his feathers, and under his wings shalt thou trust: his truth shall be thy shield and buckler" (Psalm 91:4 KJV). Men, are you too proud to have someone to lean on? Women, have you accepted the lie? Remember, both man and woman receive a covering for their sin of transgressing the Law of God.

74 In the Family

"For thou art a near kinsman." Ruth 3:9 (KJV)

A family is a group of people with an alliance, a common bond, varying in age and abilities, male and female, young and old. There is an immediate family and extended family members. Although Ruth was birthed in Moab, she was born from above, a part of the heavenly body of Christ.

Does your lifestyle resemble the family of God? Do you behave yourself in a godly way? Are your close confidants in the heavenly body? We can look into the face of our parents, children or a close relative and see similarities passed down to the descendants, in the color of hair, facial expressions, or the way we walk or talk. Can the family of God recognize you as their brother or sister? Does this world see the resemblance of Christ in you, the hope of glory? In the past we walked and talked like the world, but now that we have been called out of the world, we are to walk as Christ walked, a representative of the heavenly family of God.

Ruth identified Boaz as her near kinsman. Likewise, Christ is our near kinsman. "Now, therefore, you are no longer strangers and foreigners, but fellow citizens with the saints and members of the household of God" (Ephesians 2:19).

O that we would fashion our lives in like manner, speaking on heavenly things. "Set your mind on things above, not on things on the earth" (Colossians 3:2). Begin to identify Christ as your Lord, your God, your Savior, your Redeemer, your near kinsman. There are many today walking contrary to the call, who identify the Lord as their near kinsman. Don't be found in another man's field at harvest end only to hear the words, "I never knew you; depart from Me, you who practice lawlessness" (Matthew 7:23).

Pick of the Crop: We are identified with Christ into the heavenly family. We can be traced back to the blood of Adam and yet are born again from above. Our heritage is godly with Jesus in the pedigree. Abraham, Isaac, Jacob, Tamar, Rahab, and Ruth are all descendants of our godly ancestry. Hallelujah!

75 BLESSED BY LOVE

"Then he said, 'Blessed are you of the Lord, my daughter! For you have shown more kindness at the end than at the beginning, in that you did not go after young men, whether poor or rich.'" Ruth 3:10

God told the nation of Israel, if they would listen to Him and diligently obey His voice and all that He commands, He promised to elevate them above the nations of the world. His blessings would "overtake" them if they obeyed Him. They would be blessed in the city and field. The fruit of their body and the fruit of the ground would be blessed. They would be blessed coming in and blessed going out. Their enemy would arise from one direction and flee in seven different directions. The nations of the world would fear them. God promised to open up His good treasures, the heavens, and give rain in its season. He also promised the nation would lend and not borrow. They would be the head and not the tail. They would be above and not below. These are the blessings spoken by God to His people, if they turn not away from His words (Deuteronomy 28:1-14).

The blessings of God for His people had begun to "overtake" Ruth. And the blessings of God will "overtake" you, my friend, when you come to faith in Jesus Christ the Son of God.

The seed of love planted in Ruth's heart was bearing fruit, showing itself in kindness. God had been kind to Ruth by saving her from Moab. Ruth had been kind to Naomi, who shared the love of God with her, and Ruth showed kindness to Boaz, who had been blessing Ruth with gifts since their first meeting.

Boaz was overwhelmed by Ruth's kind words. He savored their flavor. The fruit of Ruth's heart flowed through her sweet lips and manifested itself in word and deed. Ruth sought to commit herself to Boaz, and his immediate response was, "Blessed are you of the Lord, my daughter!"

"You did not go after young men, whether poor or rich." Ruth was steadfast in her newfound love. She was on the old path, that tried and true path Jeremiah mentions: "Ask for the old paths, where the good way is, and walk in it; then you will find rest for your souls" (Jeremiah 6:16). There have been others who were offered this way of life but refused it. It's the good way leading to rest of soul for those who desire.

The young men, poor or rich, are like the new methods of drawing souls. They are attractive to the flesh, stimulating the senses. They offer health and wealth, but their message is stealth, an entertaining of flesh rather than refining of souls. Ruth preferred the old ways found only in the Ancient of Days.

Pick of the Crop: The blessings of true love will keep you on point. Love commits itself to the cause of Christ. Love's blessings prefer godly truth over earthly tares. They will seek to be rich in the poverty found in scarcity of self. This was Ruth's desire. Pray to cultivate it in your heart and mine.

76 A Godly Character

"And now, my daughter, do not fear. I will do for you all that you request, for all the people of my town know that you are a virtuous woman." Ruth 3:11

The things we do when alone gauge our character. What do you allow your eyes to behold? Where do you allow your imagination to carry you? "The wicked in his proud countenance does not seek God; God is in none of his thoughts" (Psalm 10:4). Is He in all of yours or mine? Whatever has your imagination has you, and it will shape your character for better or for worse.

"… for all the people of my town know that you are a virtuous woman." Ruth was like a marvelously smelling mandrake of the meadow, a fountain in the desert, a candle in the night, "a word spoken in due season" (Proverbs 15:23). Her character was Christ-like; God occupied her thoughts. He had become her motive. All the people of Bethlehem were blessed by her presence. She traveled to Bethlehem for a blessing and became a blessing. Don't let your culture create your character. Let Christ perform His work.

"Do not fear." Those are comforting words to a soul seeking rest in the night. Boaz covered Ruth's body with his cloak, comforted her heart with his words, and protected her image by his proclamation.

"I will do for you all you request." Boaz agreed to marry Ruth, elevating her standing far beyond that of a widow. He would stand up in her place and mediate her cause.

A vessel is worth the price paid. Diamonds scattered among the stones of earth are nothing more than stones themselves trampled by the soles of men. Only when found and ransomed is there value. "But God demonstrates His own love toward us, in that while we were still sinners, Christ died for us" (Romans 5:8).

In the depth of Christ's love for our souls, He found us among the stones of earth. He paid the ultimate price while we were yet among the mire. Boaz's love for Ruth teaches us every soul has value in God's economy. Boaz was willing to pay the full price for Ruth's redemption, resurrecting the name of Elimelech while blessing Naomi's desire to find rest for Ruth.

"Do not fear. I will do for you all that you request." The one who inhabits eternity, whose name is Holy, He is willing to mediate our plight. He took our place in death, and He will stand in our place at the judgment. It's the simplicity of the gospel in view here: if you confess Him, He will confess you. Ruth made her confession of faith in Boaz, and he confessed his love for her.

"For all the people of my town know that you are a virtuous woman." Boaz's vision of Ruth was clearly seen, though it was night. She was a virtuous woman. There are two verses in all the Bible that gives merit to someone and something that's "above rubies": wisdom (Job 28:18) and a virtuous woman (Proverbs 31:10). Ruth embodied both.

Pick of the Crop: Your thought life will tell who you are, if you're striving for godliness or slipping in sin. The battle within is manifested without, and in time the casualties are counted. God is pleased with the ways of Christ alone. When He looks at you, does He see the impression of His son or an image of yourself? Ruth's character was something Boaz delighted to join, and if Christ is in you in word and deed, He will show in your character.

YOUR THOUGHTS

77 What Is Between You and God?

"And now it is true that I am thy near kinsman: howbeit there is a kinsman nearer than I. Stay this night, and in the morning it shall be that if he will perform the duty of a close relative for you—good; let him do it. But if he does not want to perform the duty for you, then I will perform the duty for you, as the Lord lives! Lie down until morning." Ruth 3:12–13

With this news, the night grew darker for Ruth. She had traveled this night with the hope of securing an engagement, and now her desires were all but severed. Boaz was so attentive to his harvest and laborers. He was diligent, swift, strong, and prompt on every detail of his calling. With gentle correction, he alerted Ruth to another kinsman closer than he. Who could this be? What was his name? Whoever he was, he stood as a mountain between Boaz and Ruth. This barrier separating Ruth and Boaz was where fear, doubt, and unbelief would seek opportunity to insert themselves.

What is it between you and God: family, profession, lifestyle, or religion? The cares of this world will slowly choke out the Word of God from the followers of God (Mark 4:19).

The cares of this life begin to take priority within us, occupying our thoughts and time. Your day begins with a seed named distraction involving people, events, issues, and various things aimed to divert your attention away from God and His Christ.

You seem to have no time to start your day quietly, still and focused on God and His Word. As the noon time approaches, you're now engulfed in your daily activities, giving all of your emotional and mental effort that could have been given to the Giver of life. Night creeps up, and though you try to settle down at home, the phone rings, the television flickers, and computers distract ceaselessly. What is it between you and God? Most of us are unaware of the distraction.

Have you experienced similar trials? Has an obstacle come between you and God, an impediment that's keeping you from the desire of your heart? During such times, the unbridled imagination will run frantically, attempting to seek familiar ground where it seems to have more control over difficult circumstances. For Ruth, the best option was to remain still with Boaz.

"This is the work of God, that you believe in Him whom He sent" (John 6:29). God brings us to a state where, having done all that we can, we now must trust Him to work His wonders.

What is between you and God? For Adam, it was his wife (Genesis 3:17). For Esau, it was his appetite (Genesis 25:33–34). For Achan, covetousness (Joshua 7:21) and for Samson, uncontrolled sexual passions (Judges 13–16).

Pick of the Crop: The more your passion for God grows, the more He identifies obstacles preventing your intimate fellowship with Him. This is the lesson seen with Boaz and Ruth. Boaz agreed to the marriage but wanted to be assured there was nothing that would hinder their love. The same holds true with God's love. He will identify those things that stand between you and Him, things we've overlooked due to our dullness of sight.

78 Stay This Night

Don't run off in worry, Ruth. The night is dark. Where else will you turn? Remain here with me. This is what Boaz asked her, and she had to choose.

Examine the teaching of Christ. He invited His disciples to tarry the night with Him in the garden of Gethsemane (Matthew 26:31–46), and He delights to tarry with you through the dark times in your life.

"I will perform the duty for you, as the Lord lives!" Again Boaz comforted her. He invited her to pass through the night with him. He would search out the nearer relative to give him the option of redemption. "As the Lord lives," that is, as sure as God is alive, I will find this nearer kinsman and reveal his intent toward you. Boaz had faith in a favorable outcome and continued to comfort her.

She trusted in the God of Naomi, leaving Moab for Bethlehem. She trusted in the law of God to provide for a widow and a stranger by entering into the field of Boaz to reap. She trusted in the counsel of Naomi on how to approach Boaz in the night, and then she trusted Boaz to perform his part as a kinsman.

To pass back through the dark night without confirmation would be devastating. But to stay the night with the one you so desire would set at ease the longing soul.

> Until the day breaks
> And the shadows flee away,
> I will go my way to the mountain of myrrh
> And to the hill of frankincense. (Song of Solomon 4:6)

A Shulamite woman found comfort in the night, imagining a mountain of sweet myrrh and delicious smelling odors from a hill, a picture of strength that surrounds her lover.

Boaz has given his word. He's a mighty man with great abilities, and if need be he would move a mountain to redeem this Moabite woman.

"Heaven and earth will pass away, but My words will by no means pass away" (Matthew 24:35). "God is not a man, that He should lie, nor a son of man, that He should repent. Has He said, and will He not do? Or has He spoken, and will He not make it good?" (Numbers 23:19).

Pick of the Crop: As a mother comforts her restless child in the night, so too is Christ's presence to comfort all who seek Him in the dark times. If the night prevents the day, then in the presence of the Lord of the harvest, there is comfort. And when the new day dawns, His mercy and compassion are renewed. Great is His faithfulness (Lamentations 3:22–23).

79 Rest at Christ's Feet

"So she lay at his feet until morning, and she arose before one could recognize another. Then he said, 'Do not let it be known that the woman came to the threshing floor.'" Ruth 3:14

Mountains of toiling cannot outweigh
A moment of rest at Christ's feet when we lay.

At the feet of Christ is where rest is found. Cease from your labors of mind, manifesting in fleshly deeds, and rest the night in Him for there's joy in the morning.

- Jairus and a leper fell at Christ's feet (Mark 5:22, Luke 17:12–17).
- A bleeding woman was healed at Christ's feet (Mark 5:25–34).
- Mary of Bethany favored Christ's feet (Luke 10:39, John 12:3).
- And a man with departing devils sat at Christ's feet (Luke 8:35).

These all found unspeakable rest and a release of physical and mental wrestling that had tormented their souls.

Imagine the greatness of God in Christ who declares, "Heaven *is* My throne, and earth *is* My footstool" (Isaiah 66:1). Who are we to come before this awesome God full of pride? The humble in heart will be exalted. At the feet of Christ is where worship, contentment, service, and healing are found. At the feet of Christ is where we're built up and strengthen. If you're serving another, you're worshipping the works of man that cannot save.

Man exalted himself when he went against the knowledge of God and fell out of favor with the Almighty. Now he must take the position of humility and bow down in the presence of Christ. We are at His feet because we have needs in this brief life, needs only Christ can meet. Wherever you may be on your journey, take this moment and make the feet of Christ your resting place.

Pick of the Crop: Compare a restless soul to a soul at rest. Martha was upright and active. Mary was still and attentive. Martha had concerns over her circumstances. Mary was mindful of the Messiah. Martha labored, while Mary lounged, a needful thing which should not be taken away from her (Luke 10:38–42). In what position do you find yourself when in the presence of our Lord? Pray to God to direct you to the feet of Christ Jesus and they're find rest.

80 Guard Yourself Against Unseemly Opportunities

"Do not let it be known that the woman came to the threshing floor." Ruth 3:14

Many who are unchaste "have made love for hire on every threshing floor" (Hosea 9:1). It's tragic to witness ministries that have been toppled by an ill-advised visitor in and around the threshing floor of the House of God, offering the world an opportunity to blaspheme His Holy name. Keep in mind, "He leads me in the paths of righteousness for His name's sake" (Psalm 23:3). The name of God and His holy reputation is on the line when we take His name in vain with words and deeds.

Men and women in ministry from pulpit to pew, proceed with caution. Do not give your adversary any opportunity to accuse you or cause you to fall through an inappropriate relationship. You've been called to represent Christ. Can you not see the danger of improprieties behind closed quarters?

Consider this one trapping of the flesh: Hophni and Phinehas, two men, brothers and priests in their day, officiating the service of God's temple (1 Samuel 1:3). Both Hophni and Phinehas thought lightly of their service to God and were labeled sons of Belial, that is to say, sons of the devil. They were corrupt and knew not the Lord (1 Samuel 2:12). Among their many vile acts, the two would lie with the women that gathered at the door of God's House (1 Samuel 2:22). These men fell in battle (1 Samuel 4:11), but not without leaving their mark. They caused the people to abhor the offering of the Lord (1 Samuel 2:17).

The same holds true in the world today. There are laborers ministering today who cause the people of the world to abhor the offerings of the Lord with their promiscuity. The offering of the Lord is Jesus. When a minister falls by an immoral act, the media is quick to lift him up before us to showcase a staggering preacher for the sole purpose of causing the people of this current age to abhor Jesus Christ, God's offering.

Samson was physically the strongest man ever to be recorded in God's Word, called to serve God and the Hebrew people during the days when the judges ruled. In Judges 13–16, you'll find the mighty Samson plowed lower than an acre of corn by a woman. Among men he was immovable, but women found him easy to push around. He escaped the edge of men's swords only to find his head trapped on the chopping block of a woman's lap.

People of the world would have misinterpreted seeing Ruth down at the threshing floor. Those of us in the ministry of God must bear in mind we are an extension of God in this life, therefore, "give no offense in anything, that our ministry may not be blamed" (2 Corinthians 6:3).

Pick of the Crop: The world seeks opportunities to rain reproach against the name of God and the ministry. Controversies seed prideful contentions that will grow like weeds in an unattended field. When the shoots are fully matured, they will pollinate, giving rise to blasphemies against our Lord. The world has an image of how they believe the followers of Christ should live. In most cases, they are in error. Don't give the world more reason to rail against the righteous.

81 Bring the Veil and Hold It

"Also he said, 'Bring the shawl [or veil] that is on you and hold it.' And when she held it, he measured six ephahs of barley, and laid it on her. Then she went into the city." Ruth 3:15

Boaz removed his garment to spread over Ruth for a covering. This act was for her benefit, and now Boaz asked Ruth to remove her veil.

A failure to remove her veil would hinder the development of the soul. Ask yourself what blemish are you attempting to hide that He wants to reveal? Is it worth missing a blessing from His hands?

"But made Himself of no reputation, taking the form of a bondservant, and coming in the likeness of men" (Philippians 2:7). The King of kings took off His robe of glory and became a servant of servants in the form of a man. Can you see the picture? Heaven's glory disrobed and donned earth's depravity so that we might be covered with His robe.

Naked was He born into this world, adorned in heaven's acclaim!
Naked He died for this world, clothed with sinners' shame.

"For He made Him who knew no sin to be sin for us, that we might become the righteousness of God in Him" (2 Corinthians 5:21).

Never deny God an opportunity to bless you when you're required to remove someone or something from your life. Again, it's for our good. The king of Nineveh removed his royal robe in an act of humility to plead for national salvation, "and he arose from his throne and laid aside his robe, covered himself with sackcloth and sat in ashes" (Jonah 3:6). The removal of Lazarus' grave clothes was necessary for the man who was passing from death to newness of life. "Jesus said to them, 'Loose him, and let him go'" (John 11:44). The apostle Paul wrote to Ephesian believers, "that you put off, concerning your former conduct, the old man which grows corrupt according to the deceitful lusts, and be renewed in the spirit of your mind, and that you put on the new man which was created according to God, in true righteousness and holiness" (Ephesians 4:22–24).

How many times in our lives have we delayed or even prevented Christ from unveiling and stripping our deeds in the flesh? Had not Ruth removed her veil, she would not have the wherewithal to receive a blessing from Boaz.

Pick of the Crop: What are the methods you have used to conceal your fleshly desires? Christ asks us to remove that veil, exposing more of ourselves to Him for His work to proceed. You must trust Him through this process, which will reap great rewards. Ask the Lord to help you remove anything that is not of God and trust Christ to bless your soul in return.

82 UNVEILED

A young Shulamite woman described the close relationship she desired with her lover during her dark night of faith. The closer she grew to him, the greater she was unveiled, casting aside those things in her life that stunted her growth, things that hindered her heavenly relationship.

Her lover knocked at the door of her heart, but she responded slowly. Her lover called out to her, and yet she was slow to open up to him. Finally, her sluggish soul responded to his call and she was anointed similar to Ruth. To her surprise, her lover was not to be found.

> I opened to my beloved;
> But my beloved had withdrawn himself, and was
> gone:
> My soul failed when he spake:
> I sought him, but I could not find him;
> I called him, but he gave me no answer.
> (Song of Solomon 5:6 KJV)

Why would her lover approach only to withdraw? She was anointed. She desired only him. All this was true; however, another layer of unveiling was necessary.

She continued, "The watchmen that went about the city found me, they smote me, they wounded me; the keepers of the walls took away my veil from me" (Song of Solomon 5:7 KJV). Her unveiling came at the hands of the watchmen, the keepers of the wall—that is to say, those who give warning, ministers of God! Why would God allow this group to take part in her unveiling? One lesson is this: man in all his best intentions is flawed. True love, a true union of the soul, is found only in Christ, the lover of souls.

True, God's stripping us of our former covering is painfully uncomfortable to our flesh, but it's needed for our advancement.

Pick of the Crop: When the man and the woman were joined together, both were naked and not ashamed (Genesis 2:25). As the result of sin, we sought a covering to hide ourselves from a sinless God. Now God seeks to bring everyone back to a sinless state in Him through Christ Jesus, but we must be willing to unveil ourselves completely without reservations that we might be clothed in the righteousness of Christ.

83 Hold Out Your Veil

"Bring the shawl [or veil] that is on you and hold it." That is, hold it out before Christ. Seize it. Take hold of it. Lift it up before Him where He can begin to do His work. You cannot receive the blessings He has in store until you do your part. Holding it out before you is a full confession, exposing yourself to Christ.

There was a man with a shriveled, paralyzed, and withered hand in the synagogue (Mark 3:1–5). The hand had no use. The man could not write, labor, nor produce anything with that hand. There was nothing of value about that hand until Christ asked him to stretch it out. We have similar things that are now a part of our lives, things we have had close to us for years. They're dead works for the most part. We receive no true value from them.

But when God appeared in our lives and asked us to stretch out our withered work and hold it out before Him, we began to see His working in those dead areas that have hindered us for years.

What are you holding on to, that thing that has hindered your advancement in life and in Christ? It's crippling you. Think about it. We keep so many things close to the breast, things Christ wants to remove and make a change for our good. But the separation is the fearful part. Separate yourself from the familiar ways you've grown into, ways of life, habits, communication, old practices, old relationships, and give these things over to Christ. Hold them out before Him. Distance yourself from them, and watch God take those things, those areas of your life, and do a marvelous work.

"And when she held it, he measured six ephahs of barley, and laid it on her. Then she went into the city." When the Lord of the harvest asks us to unveil, it's His stripping, His pruning for our good, that we may bring forth more fruit. "Every branch that bears fruit He prunes, that it may bear more fruit," more life-giving seed carried to its rightful place (John 15:2). There was a blessing that followed the night.

Ruth learned obedience, and no matter how painful obedience may be, it has its rewards.

Pick of the Crop: Whatever your veil may be, the command is given to hold it. The veil that held you, that thing which overlaid your every emotion, now is held by you through the power of the Lord's command. He has given you authority to remove that which has bound you and to seize it, remembering that His power within you does the work.

84 Emptied of Ourselves

"When she came to her mother-in-law, she said, 'Is that you, my daughter?' Then she told her all that the man had done for her. And she said, 'These six ephahs of barley he gave me; for he said to me, "Do not go empty-handed to your mother-in-law."'" Ruth 3:16–17

Ruth returned to the city a different woman. She eagerly explained all that took place. Her veil had been removed, and she was bearing the burden of Boaz's barley seeds, a prophetic symbol.

"Do not go empty-handed to your mother-in-law." The night brought about a complete emptying of Ruth. This is the place in our lives where God delights for us to be, completely emptied of our will that His will might be done. What are our talents or possessions to God? We don't make God anymore god-like by our works and abilities. He's not any better off by something you or I own. God seeks to empty us.

He was in the beginning. "Before the mountains were brought forth, or ever You had formed the earth and the world, even from everlasting to everlasting, You are God" (Psalm 90:2). He always has been and always will be. When Moses inquired about the name of God before presenting himself to the people of God, he heard, "I AM WHO I AM. . . . Thus you shall say to the children of Israel, 'I AM has sent me to you'" (Exodus 3:14). The God-Man repeats this thought while contending with the Jews. "Most assuredly, I say to you, before Abraham was, I AM" (John 8:58). He is self-existing.

God needs nothing. Ruth's emptying assured her refilling with Boaz's gift to carry to Naomi as a blessing. We want to be able to bless the people of God with the blessings that come from God and not of ourselves. God's church in this world has a role in the blessing of God's people, the nation of Israel, and we should never grow empty-handed toward them, for therein lies a blessing for us.

Ruth shared her blessings with her mother-in-law. We should exercise every opportunity to care for the aged. Naomi's labors had not been in vain in the Lord. Since her return to Bethlehem, she reaped and would continue to reap from Ruth's work. What a difference a harvest brings in the lives of God's people. "Therefore be patient, brethren, until the coming of the Lord. See how the farmer waits for the precious fruit of the earth, waiting patiently for it until it receives the early and latter rain. You also be patient. Establish your hearts, for the coming of the Lord is at hand" (James 5:7–8).

The examples of Naomi and Ruth offer valuable lessons for us to remain close to Christ in our journey through difficult times. When it looks like there's no possible way out of your troubles and your sorrow, you must not give up on God.

> But also for this very reason, giving all diligence, add to your faith virtue, to virtue knowledge, to knowledge self-control, to self-control perseverance, to perseverance godliness, to godliness brotherly kindness, and to brotherly kindness love. For if these things are yours and abound, you will be neither barren nor unfruitful in the knowledge of our Lord Jesus Christ. (2 Peter 1:5–8)

Pick of the Crop: I suppose the emptying of ourselves is one of the most difficult tasks there is to perform. That translates into the death of our desires and becoming completely alive to Christ in all that we do. Enoch was such a man, so alive to the presence of God that God took him in to heaven. “He had this testimony, that he pleased God” (Hebrews 11:5). Elijah was also an empty vessel, so alive to the Spirit of God that God took him up into heaven, not seeing physical death as we know it (2 Kings 2:11). With man, the emptying of ourselves is an impossibility, but with God, all things are possible (Matthews 19:26).

85 Waiting on God

"Then she said, 'Sit still, my daughter, until you know how the matter will turn out; for the man will not rest until he has concluded the matter this day.'" Ruth 3:18

There will come times in this pilgrims' way when we are called to quietly wait on God, no more outward activity of the flesh or inward wrestling of soul. You, in all your efforts, have done that which is required. You fasted, prayed, and separated yourself to God. You sang songs of Zion with a heavy heart. You sought the counsel of God as one seeks fine gold. Now there's one thing left to do: sit still.

"Be still, and know that I am God" (Psalm 46:10). Give God a chance to show Himself marvelously in your life by simply waiting on Him to do what He said He'll do. Step aside. "My soul, wait silently for God alone, for my expectation is from Him" (Psalm 62:5). Those are the divinely inspired words of David who had a confidence in God to be envied. Be still. Be still. Be still.

"The man will not rest until he has concluded the matter this day." Boaz would not rest until his mission of redeeming Ruth and Naomi was complete. Here again is a picture of Jesus Christ, the most driven man to walk this earth. He was God-focused, God-centered. He would not relent in His role as Redeemer. His rest came at His resurrection and presentation of His blood before the Father. Until that hour, Christ would say, "My food is to do the will of Him who sent Me, and to finish His work" (John 4:34).

"For I have come down from heaven, not to do My own will, but the will of Him who sent Me" (John 6:38).

"For the Lord God will help Me; therefore I will not be disgraced; therefore I have set My face like a flint, and I know that I will not be ashamed" (Isaiah 50:7).

With the same God-breathed confidence, Boaz set out to finish the task at hand.

Pick of the Crop: A finite creature attempts to wait on an infinite God only with difficulty. Man is subject to time, but time is subject to God who has put eternity in our hearts, teaching us to think in those terms (Ecclesiastes 3:11). "Rest in the LORD, and wait patiently for him" (Psalm 37:7).

YOUR THOUGHTS

MARRIAGE OF THE SOUL

86 THE GATES OF RIGHTEOUSNESS

"Then went Boaz up to the gate, and sat him down there: and, behold, the kinsman of whom Boaz spake came by; unto whom he said, Ho, such a one! turn aside, sit down here. And he turned aside, and sat down." Ruth 4:1 (KJV)

Up to the gate Boaz went and sat down. The gate was the place where:

- the elders of the city with honor and authority met,
- appointments for officers and judges were made,
- court was held (Deuteronomy 16:18–19),
- the prophets preached righteousness (Jeremiah 17:19–20),
- the resounding roll of Wisdom's proclamations were heard (Proverbs 1:20–21),
- the people of the city gathered to hear the reading of the Law of God (Nehemiah 8:1–3).

"Open to me the gates of righteousness: I will go into them, and I will praise the LORD" (Psalm 118:19 KJV). The gates stood to represent righteousness for all who entered, invoking praise to God.

Imagine those gates in glory opening like the arms of a friend spreading to welcome a loved one with tender embrace. The gates of righteousness are opened at the request of those who have been made righteous by the King of Righteousness. "But outside are dogs and sorcerers and sexually immoral and murderers and idolaters, and whoever loves and practices a lie" (Revelation 22:15). Don't expect to be part of God's fellowship on high while practicing lawlessness here below. Heaven is a gated community.

The gate was the place where the widow would come and cry for justice, seeking mediation for redemption by a willing kinsman if her husband died leaving her without sons to continue the family name (Deuteronomy 25:5–10). Ruth was noticeably absent; Boaz stood in her place.

Here again, the same principle is true in our lives. Christ stands before the throne of God in our stead. Jesus is present to plead.

Job sought for someone who would mediate his plight, try his case, or stand in his place. "Nor is there any mediator between us, who may lay his hand on us both" (Job 9:33). The man whom Job longed for has come in the person of Jesus Christ, "for there is one God and one Mediator between God and men, the Man Christ Jesus" (1 Timothy 2:5). Boaz knew the heart of God and the heart of Ruth. He was a stellar man, known in the land, and he had a delightful plan for Ruth waiting to be revealed.

Pick of the Crop: O Lord my God, open to me your gates of righteousness that I may enter in and praise your holy name. May mercy and truth flow from my heart to proclaim your Word in all the earth.

87 THE EXPOSING OF SELF

Early morning is a busy time in and around Bethlehem. As the sun continues to grow in the sky, so too the people populating the city streets with the merchants.

Boaz, now seated in his place at the gate, is watchful. Hidden among the multitude is the near-kinsman in question. Boaz quickly identifies him, understanding his devices. He is familiar with all the ways of this near-kinsman and his subtleness of heart. He moves in and out among the crowd, traveling to and fro in the land unexpectedly. He is crafty with a low regard for the law, people, and souls.

"Ho, such a one! turn aside, sit down here."

Boaz draws him out. This near-kinsman has no power to resist the command.

Who is he? He is the self. Our self-will is that nearer kinsman. Sin flows through mankind as blood through capillaries. There is not any area of our being where sin has not reached. Sin fuels the flesh, energizing self-will with venomous filth. "For I know that in me (that is, in my flesh) nothing good dwells" (Romans 7:18).

Our self-will is so closely woven into our souls we often forget he's present. During our lives in Moab, self-will went unnoticed, and in Bethlehem, Naomi overlooked this near-kinsman. Ruth, a novice, had no knowledge of him, and neither had we. It took Boaz to identify this near-kinsman. He called him out of the shadows into the light. The same is true when Christ is in our lives; only Christ, our kinsman, can reveal the heart of self-will in all of us.

Self-will is intractable and insidious, especially when we're prompted by the Spirit of God to do a deed designed to identify our self-will.

Christ delights to weaken and destroy all selfishness in the lives of His people.

Through the course of a day we may offend a sister or brother. The Spirit of God, with gentle conviction and with words only He knows, communicates to our spirit to go apologize to the offended. It may be a spouse, a child, a relative, a coworker, or a friend. It doesn't matter who it is; we've been commanded to go. The strength of our self-will dictates our obedience to the Lord or not. Beloved, this should not be the case.

Self controls most areas of our lives instead of Christ. When obedience is delayed, it gives self an opportunity to deceive. It grows and transforms into self-deception and self-justification. Remember this, obedience delayed is obedience denied.

Pick of the Crop: The subtleties of our selfish life have multiple layers that enclose us as a husk over an ear of corn. Only the Lord of the harvest can pull away the coverings of self. As self is exposed and discarded, it begins to reveal the king's kernel, full of delicious, life-giving seed. This process will manifest in you as the layers of self fall away.

88 The Beautiful Crimson Door

Self-will and the Savior are not symbiotic. Christ and the cesspool of self cannot coexist. Self-actualization, self-realization, and self-esteem are not the way into peace with God in His home on high.

There was a mighty man who had a son. He built a great house surrounded by a great wall. At the front of the wall stood a door made of the finest cedar. The man's son was mortally wounded while building this house, spilling his blood, but he still lives. The son fashioned the door covering it with the most costly crimson ever, mingling it with his precious blood as a testimony to his father and for their love of people. Passersby would stop to gaze upon this door in awe of its beauty. There was none like it in all the land. This door graced the mighty man's estate welcoming all who sought to enter in.

The mighty man sent messengers throughout the land informing the inhabitants he was having a great feast in honor of his great son, who though mortally wounded still lived and had finished the work his father had given him to do. Everyone was welcome, the only stipulation being that all must enter through the glorious, crimson door.

When all things were made ready, the mighty man sent out a trumpet player who blew a great sound announcing the start of the great feast. The door was opened, and a great light from the mighty man's great wealth and glory and honor and power and joy and peace and love covered the land, reaching into the darkest places. The light was as the morning dew upon the tender grass shoots, as rain upon a barren land. "The people which sat in darkness saw great light; and to them which sat in the region and shadow of death light is sprung up" (Matthew 4:16 KJV).

Many people were seen arriving at the door of the mighty man's home in varying conditions. There were the very old and the very young. The blind and the lame came. An amazing thing happened when any man or woman entered through the door. All their infirmities were removed as they passed the door. The rich, the few who entered, were made equal to the poor, as if riches and poverty were nothing. Multitudes flocked into the home, and yet there was room for more.

Servants made a final sweep of the country and found people who no man had considered nor loved, and yet they had room for still more. At the word of the mighty man, the time for the closing of the door arrived. His son came forward and looked out into the distance. One final soul was seen approaching. The son waited for his guest to enter, welcoming him. Before closing the door, the son soberly looked out over the vast land, hoping for just one more. His father assured him the invitations had reached every living soul. The son paused one last time and finally shut the door, closing the land in great darkness.

Within there was feasting and celebrating like never before. Every tear was wiped away. The beauty of the house within the walls was indescribable.

During the celebration the mighty man and his son were informed by those who kept watch that some had attempted to enter the house by climbing the wall. The mighty man went to them and said, "My son waited for you by the door, but you refused to enter that way? Am I not the master of this house? Take all those who sought to enter in another way and cast them out into the darkness."

You, likewise, would have little regard for the man or woman who has been invited to your home but insists on entering through a window. Jesus said, "I am the door. If anyone enters by Me, he will be saved, and will go in and out and find pasture" (John 10:9).

Pick of the Crop: I passed through that crimson door, which bid me to come out of the night into his light full of glory and delights. Your passage into the new life can begin while in your present body, by simply crossing over the threshold He laid down.

89 Jesus, the Door into God's Kingdom

Jesus is the door to God's kingdom. All other selfish attempts are futile. God does not want to send souls to hell, but God will execute His righteous judgment and cast out those who rebel (Luke 12:5). The world is self-seeking, self-propagating, self-absorbed, self-loving, self-centered, self-serving, and self-gratifying with self- preservation in mind. We're all selfish. When man lives on God's earth for himself and attempts to climb up to God's heavenly home by his own means, he is nothing more than a selfish creature.

Consider how great God is, who spoke the heavens and all that is visible and invisible into existence. "For by Him all things were created that are in heaven and that are on earth, visible and invisible, whether thrones or dominions or principalities or powers. All things were created through Him and for Him. And He is before all things, and in Him all things consist." (Colossians 1:16–17). It is the pride of man who thinks he could approach God on merit.

At His command, that which was not came into being. A fig tree failed at the sound of His voice. "'Let no fruit grow on you ever again.' Immediately the fig tree withered away" (Matthew 21:19). Soaring seas became serene at His word. "He arose and rebuked the wind and the raging of the water. And they ceased, and there was a calm" (Luke 8:24). The spirit world obeys Him. "Jesus rebuked him, saying, 'Be quiet, and come out of him!' And when the unclean spirit had convulsed him and cried out with a loud voice, he came out of him" (Mark 1:25–26). Death gave up the dead at Christ's demand. "He took the child by the hand, and said to her, 'Talitha, cumi,' which is translated, 'Little girl, I say to you, arise.' Immediately the girl arose and walked" (Mark 5:41–42).

The powers of God have a portal. His name is Jesus. If you want to experience His kingdom glory, it is only possible through His Son.

Search the Scriptures; all creation obeys the voice of God, except the rebellious heart of sinful man. Man is the only creature who refuses to obey the Almighty, Eternal God.

Read closely the word that leads the list of the condition of humanity in the last days. "For men will be lovers of themselves, lovers of money, boasters, proud, blasphemers, disobedient to parents, unthankful, unholy, unloving, unforgiving, slanderers, without self-control, brutal, despisers of good, traitors, headstrong, haughty, lovers of pleasure rather than lovers of God, having a form of godliness but denying its power. And from such people turn away!" (2 Timothy 3:2–5). God will not have the above lifestyles in His dwelling place.

We must exercise a life of self-denial or risk being denied by the Crucified. "If anyone desires to come after Me, let him deny himself, and take up his cross daily, and follow Me" (Luke 9:23). There's an unsearchable number of ways self can surface in this life of ours. Praise God for Boaz, and praise God for Christ. Christ is a firm foundation for our feet and hope for our hearts.

Pick of the Crop: On this side of the door, you'll encounter pains and sufferings. On the other side of the door, there's joy and peace. This side, death; the other side, life eternal. This side of the door, mortality rules; on the other side, immortality reigns. On this side, contending with the flesh; on the other side, a continuation of the spirit. The door of death will be entered. It's best to go through the way of Christ.

90 Self-Will and Religion

Our Lord identified the self-will of sin's intent within Cain, Adam's son. "So the Lord said to Cain, 'Why are you angry? And why has your countenance fallen? If you do well, will you not be accepted? And if you do not do well, sin lies at the door. And its desire is for you, but you should rule over it'" (Genesis 4:6–7).

God has given mankind authority and has commanded them to rule over sin's self-will. Read the account of Cain closely, slowly, prayerfully in Genesis 4:1–7. Sin's desire is to control us. How is this done? Through our self-will. On the other hand, our Lord has instructed us to rule over sin. The only way to achieve victory over sin is to approach God on the terms found in the sacrifice He requires.

Cain wanted approval from God for his own religious ceremony contrary to God's desire for him. His heart was not right. God instructed him to look toward the coming Messiah, our Savior Jesus Christ, but Cain rejected God's plan. God desired fellowship with him in spirit, but Cain refused God's way of worship.

Since the fall of man, the sinful heart of self has resisted God's love at every turn. "But these speak evil of whatever they do not know; and whatever they know naturally, like brute beasts, in these things they corrupt themselves. Woe to them! For they have gone in the way of Cain" (Jude 10–11). The way of Cain is self-religion, man's attempt to approach God by religious means. The religious fruit of man's hands can never save.

Self is situated high in the religious circle of today's world. In the name of religion, it offers to God works of the flesh, sustained by pompous platitudes which pacify only for a moment. There's little change in the heart and soul of men and women who come to God through religious ceremonies. They offer the fruit of the ground that was cursed, things that are sweet to the taste and soothing to the ears, rather than the bitterness of death through a blood offering, which points to Christ. In the name of religion, self will go to the extreme as long as Christ is eliminated from its ceremonies. "Not by works of righteousness which we have done, but according to His mercy He saved us, through the washing of regeneration and renewing of the Holy Spirit" (Titus 3:5). The works of religion cannot save. Only through the tender mercies of Christ will we stand without blemish before God. Boaz knows the near-kinsman's selfish ways and will soon expose them to the people.

Pick of the Crop: It's not the religion that saves, that is, ceremonious rituals. Rather it's the relationship you have with the living God. How well do you know God the Father in Christ Jesus? Are you intimate enough with Him to obey His voice?

91 Self-Will and Salvation

Jonah, the prophet of God, had huge self-will issues. He built a booth to bear witness to Nineveh's destruction, but God wanted their deliverance. "Then God saw their works, that they turned from their evil way; and God relented from the disaster that He had said He would bring upon them, and He did not do it" (Jonah 3:10). The heart of God proclaims, "For I have no pleasure in the death of one who dies . . . Therefore turn and live!" (Ezekiel 18:32).

Notice God exposing the self-will within His prophet:

> Then God said to Jonah, "Is it right for you to be angry about the plant?"
>
> And he said, "It is right for me to be angry, even to death!"
>
> But the Lord said, "You have had pity on the plant for which you have not labored, nor made it grow, which came up in a night and perished in a night. And should I not pity Nineveh, that great city, in which are more than one hundred and twenty thousand persons who cannot discern between their right hand and their left—and much livestock?" (Jonah 4:9–11)

Salvation is a gift of God, not man (Ephesians 2:8). In the wisdom of this world, man has attempted to package salvation and distribute it according to the ways of the world. Beware of the trappings of self-will and salvation.

Jonah selfishly sought the destruction of Nineveh and pitied a plant over a people. He wanted to pick and choose where God's mercy should fall. There are shepherds, pastors, ministers, and evangelists, people standing in the place of God, who do not have the salvation of souls on their minds. Rather, they are advancing an agenda of their own reputation. We have an example of it here in Jonah. God delivered Nineveh, a sin-laden non-Jewish nation, from righteous destruction. The citizens had humbled their hearts, while the prophet hardened his. The people had repented, and the prophet rebelled. Self-will can be found hidden among the people of God, and this is also part of the makeup of the nearer kinsman.

Pick of the Crop: Self-will attempts to dictate to the author of salvation who should be saved. What a fool. "Have you an arm like God?" (Job 40:9). Self-will obscures the wisdom of God by words without knowledge (Job 38:2). Salvation is a free gift to all. Pray to God that we will never stand in a place to say who will or will not be saved.

92 Self-Will and Authority

Nathan the prophet told King David a story of a rich man and a poor man living in the same city. The rich man held a feast for a guest. Instead of selecting a lamb from the wealth of his flock, the rich man stole, killed, and served the poor man's only lamb, one that was very dear to his family.

> So David's anger was greatly aroused against the man, and he said to Nathan, "*As* the LORD lives, the man who has done this shall surely die! And he shall restore fourfold for the lamb, because he did this thing and because he had no pity."
>
> Then Nathan said to David, "You are the man!" (2 Samuel 12:5–7)

It's a wonder how David, the lover of God, walked away from holy living to serve the lust of his flesh. It took the Spirit of God through a prophet of God to reveal to this man of God his selfish deeds.

The circle of some authorities is a tightly knit knot. In there, the privileged dress themselves with robes of their own fraternities. There are few in number, yet the decisions they make are far felt. "Woe to those who decree unrighteous decrees, who write misfortune, which they have prescribed" (Isaiah 10:1).

David's inner circle knew of his sinful affair and the death of one of his warriors; David's confidants were active participants in his sin. His authority made unrighteous decisions, passed down unrighteous judgments. With ultimate authority over the land, David chose adultery and selected a side of murder. The decisions he made cost him dearly, but he would later find forgiveness from God.

If God has placed you in a position of authority, it's for God's purposes, not yours. Read the records of Jesus contending with the lawyers, scribes, Pharisees, priests, and rulers who were blinded by their self-will in the position of authority.

"Then the Pharisees went out and plotted against Him, how they might destroy Him" (Matthew 12:14). With the authority of religion, these men sought to destroy the man whose lovely hands touched the putrid flesh of a leper to make him clean (Matthew 8:3). Religion sought to bring down the lofty hands of the man that made clay to anoint the eyes of the blind to restore his sight (John 9:6—7). Religion threatened those heavenly hands that touched the dead, restoring their vitality (Mark 5:41). Everywhere He went He was doing good (Acts 10:38). The man who received His orders from the Author of authority and not from man's religious societies was alienated by those social clubs.

After the religious rulers seized and bound Christ, He was brought before Pilate, the governor of that day, who "knew that the chief priests had handed Him over because of envy" (Mark 15:10).

"When morning came, all the chief priests and elders of the people plotted against Jesus to put Him to death" (Matthew 27:1).

Self-will and religious authority have damaged and continue to ravage people around the world in the name of religion. Boaz knew this thinking was in the nearer kinsman's heart, and it concerned him.

Pick of the Crop: "My brethren, let not many of you become teachers, knowing that we shall receive a stricter judgment" (James 3:1). Those in authority ought to hunt for humility and judgment. The higher you fly the further you fall, if in error.

93 Self-Will and Riches

Riches will deceive you into thinking God's favor is on your life. Your wealth will deceive you into thinking you're walking in the ways of God. Don't be fooled. "Take heed and beware of covetousness, for one's life does not consist in the abundance of the things he possesses." (Luke 12:15).

A rich man came running to Jesus and kneeling asked what he must do to inherit life eternal. Jesus directs him to the law. The rich man said he has observed all of it from his youth. "Then Jesus, looking at him, loved him, and said to him, 'One thing you lack: Go your way, sell whatever you have and give to the poor, and you will have treasure in heaven; and come, take up the cross, and follow Me.' But he was sad at this word, and went away sorrowful, for he had great possessions" (Mark 10:21–22).

Like the man between Boaz and Ruth, one thing stood between the rich man and Jesus, self-love of riches and temporal things. The man had convinced himself he was in good standing before God and was eager to hear Christ justify him until that thing he trusted in was revealed. Christ loved the rich man and offered him everlasting, eternal riches in Heaven, far exceeding the temporal riches of this world.

By having his self exposed, the rich man was extremely saddened, so much so he literally turned his back on Jesus, the lover of his soul, and walked away. Don't let your love of riches cause you to walk away from the love of Christ. We'll come to see this nearer kinsman's love for his riches cause him to turn his back on the love of God's law and souls.

I toiled earth's wealth. All is vain,
Mining for riches that will remain.

Then Christ's treasures were granted to me.
They'll not fade tho' eternity flee.

Pick of the Crop: The deceitfulness of riches coupled with the subtleties of self may convince you that you're heaven bound when you are not. Self wants to be preserved comfortably and avoid any spiritual growth that will avert it from indulgence. Be not deceived. No pain in self-denial, no gain in heavenly treasure.

94 SELF-WILL AND GIVING

Riches and giving are a deceptive combination when self-will is involved. "For who makes you differ from another? And what do you have that you did not receive? Now if you did indeed receive it, why do you boast as if you had not received it?" (1 Corinthians 4:7). Self gives of its superfluity, but God wants our souls.

One's wealth may give them security, but there's a sensation deep within that's not satisfied. Self-deception attempts to suppress this feeling by accumulating temporal things, such as homes, cars, toys, boys, girls, pets, position, power, and any other thing that can be purchased. People of the world have given enormously to show their abundance, but that inner void can only be filled by Christ.

Our Lord sat near the temple treasury to watch how the people gave. The wealthy men made a hypocritical show of giving a small part of their abundance. A poor widow gave all that she had out of her poverty (Luke 21:1–4). In the eyes of the world, the rich men were rewarded. In the eyes of Christ, the poor gave more.

God watches how we give. "Now Jesus sat opposite the treasury and saw how the people put money into the treasury. And many who were rich put in much" (Mark 12:41). He's also concerned with what we give. Have you given God your very best? Have you? He wants the best of your time, abilities, and possessions. Remember, He is God. He gave His best for us. Shouldn't we do likewise?

Self thinks very little of giving to God the best he or she has to offer, with an ever diminishing reverence for God and His holiness. The people of God offered sacrifices on His pure altar, sacrifices that where torn, lame, and sick. "'You also say, "Oh, what a weariness!" And you sneer at it,' Says the Lord of hosts. 'And you bring the stolen, the lame, and the sick; thus you bring an offering! Should I accept this from your hand?' says the Lord" (Malachi 1:13). These types of sacrifices should not come before God. These sacrifices are second-best, with little thought and regard to the receiver of such. Self holds back the best for self. Boaz knew the near kinsman would do the same toward God, Naomi, and Ruth.

This also must be said, "Though I bestow all my goods to feed the poor, and though I give my body to be burned, but have not love, it profits me nothing" (1 Corinthians 13:3). Man cannot give the love of God through his actions without first possessing the love of God. A selfish lifestyle opposes that love.

Explore these examples of mature giving. Hannah, a woman who was childless, gave a son she didn't have to the service of God all the days of his life. "Then she made a vow and said, "O Lord of hosts, if You will indeed look on the affliction of Your maidservant and remember me, and not forget Your maidservant, but will give Your maidservant a male child, then I will give him to the Lord all the days of his life, and no razor shall come upon his head" (1 Samuel 1:11).

Paul the apostle gave Timothy, his most valued son in the faith, to the church at Philippi, "for I have no one like-minded, who will sincerely care for your state" (Philippians 2:20).

Paul's letter to the Corinthian believers boasts of the type of giving that came from the poor Macedonia churches. "And not only as we had hoped, but they first gave themselves to the Lord, and then to us by the will of God" (2 Corinthians 8:5). They demonstrated an unselfish pattern of giving, a giving that costs.

Give unselfishly to God in whatever capacity He calls you. Are you working in a ministry that assists the elderly? Give your best. Are you teaching the young sproutlets in a Sunday school class? Give your best. Are you supporting a work of God financially? Give your best.

Boaz knew he would not find this willingness to give in that nearer kinsman.

Pick of the Crop: Self can never give of a pure heart. It is contrary to its nature. Love gives freely; self gives with strings attached. Love releases its gifts to the wind, but the gifts of self are restrained.

95 SELF-WILL AND SELF-RIGHTEOUSNESS

One of the vilest manifestations of self is seen in the realm of self-righteousness. It's especially unpleasant when it appears in a representative of God. "As it is written: 'There is none righteous, no, not one'" (Romans 3:10). "But we are all like an unclean thing, and all our righteousnesses are like filthy rags" (Isaiah 64:6). True righteousness is found "through faith in Jesus Christ, to all and on all who believe" (Romans 3:22).

With that understanding, why would we allow self to surface in displays of religious revelry? You don't have to look hard to discover it within the religious mainstream and in academia.

Jesus tells a story to a group "who trusted in themselves that they were righteous, and despised others" (Luke 18:9).

There were two men, one temple. Both entered in.

Two professions: an agent for God and a steward of the world.

Two dispositions: one high, the other low.

Two postures: one erect, the other bowed.

Two spirits: one proud, the other humble.

A Pharisee (or preacher) exalted himself and prayed with himself. The publican (or tax collector) humbled himself by standing far off and prayed to God.

The preacher talked about what he was not. The tax collector confessed to God who he was.

The preacher wrapped himself in his own praise. The tax collector was enveloped in a broken and contrite heart.

The preacher, as did Lucifer, (Isaiah 14:12-14) lifted up his "I" to God. The tax collector "would not so much as raise his eyes to heaven" (Luke 18:13).

The preacher rejected the sinner, whereas the Teacher accepted the sinful believers who repented of their sins.

"But your iniquities have separated you from your God; and your sins have hidden His face from you, so that He will not hear" (Isaiah 59:2). It's our sinful self-life that separates us from God. Self is like a chameleon effortlessly blending into every area of human existence. Ask God to reveal anything that is of self within your heart and deliver you through His redeeming love. The nearer kinsman was the embodiment of the self-willed life, and he cannot stand in the judgment.

Pick of the Crop: Self-righteousness and pride are joined at the hip. When pride is humbled, self seeks to puff it up again. Should self be stricken, pride will shower it with esteem. In heaven you will not find the self-righteous alongside those made righteous through the blood of Christ.

96 Judging the Kinsman

"And he took ten men of the elders of the city, and said, 'Sit down here.' So they sat down.

"Then he said to the close relative, 'Naomi, who has come back from the country of Moab, sold the piece of land which belonged to our brother, Elimelech. And I thought to inform you, saying, "Buy it back in the presence of the inhabitants and the elders of my people. If you will redeem it, redeem it; but if you will not redeem it, then tell me, that I may know; for there is no one but you to redeem it, and I am next after you."'

"And he said, 'I will redeem it.'" Ruth 4:2–4

Ten men, elders who represented the law of government, were assembled. They would oversee the matter of Naomi and Ruth. The twelve men were seated, and the nearer kinsman would have his love of the law tested.

There are many in the Christian camp who talk a good talk. They know when to stand or sit, when to lift up their hands and shout, and when to say amen, but there's coming a day when "by your words you will be justified, and by your words you will be condemned" (Matthew 12:37). According to your ways will you be judged (Ezekiel 24:14). Your love of the Lord and His people will be made known. The nearer kinsman's day had come.

Boaz began, "Naomi, who has come back from the country of Moab . . ." Boaz stated Naomi is no longer bound by the meals of Moab. Her appetites are met in Bethlehem. She was dead and now alive; she was lost and now found.

It's difficult to imagine the nearer kinsman without this knowledge. We were informed "all the city was excited because of them" (Ruth 1:19). Word spread quickly, like fire through a field, concerning Naomi's return with a Moabite. Bethlehem was the smallest of the cities within the tribe of Judah, so one woman's business was the whole town's business. For the purpose of formalities and for the sake of the people who had now gathered, Boaz revealed the details.

The hidden motives of our hearts are seen and understood by God. Motives may be concealed for a time, but our actions declare our motives and we are judged by humanity. "But the LORD shall endure forever; He has prepared His throne for judgment. He shall judge the world in righteousness, and He shall administer judgment for the peoples in uprightness" (Psalm 9:7-8).

Pick of the Crop: All will be given righteous judgment before God and His Christ. We will give an account of ourselves (Romans 14:12). The motives of the kinsman's heart will be judged, and so will yours and mine. All humanity will have to answer for the way they lived on this earth. You'll never know when you'll be called out. Will you be ready?

97 The Order: First Man, Second Man

"And he said unto the kinsman, Naomi, that is come again out of the country of Moab, selleth a parcel of land, which was our brother Elimelech's." Ruth 4:3 (KJV)

The issue of Naomi's land was the first point to be examined. It was available for redemption, that is, purchase. Boaz informed the kinsman about Naomi's plight and waited on his response.

God's love of humanity has given His gift of free will. With free will comes an immeasurable amount of responsibility to govern ourselves. How do we control our bodies?

Control is evident by the disciplined thought life, keeping watch over the words we speak and demonstrating dominion over the actions of the flesh, things that are not pleasing in the sight of God. We have a choice to lie, steal, kill, fornicate, or commit adultery. We also have the choice to speak a pleasant word, think pleasant thoughts, or do helpful deeds. The free will of man is demonstrated even among the young before a child can walk or talk. "But I discipline my body and bring it into subjection, lest, when I have preached to others, I myself should become disqualified" (1 Corinthians 9:27).

God gave mankind free will to exercise as each individual chooses. The natural man, self-will, has an affectionate love for the things of this world. Self-will primarily wants to fulfill selfish desires that feed the flesh. In the Garden of Eden, Adam and Eve's self-will, free to obey God, chose to go against Him. "So when the woman saw that the tree *was* good for food, that it *was* pleasant to the eyes, and a tree desirable to make *one* wise, she took of its fruit and ate. She also gave to her husband with her, and he ate" (Genesis 3:6).

Until Christ is seated on the thrown of our will, the natural man, self-will, always surfaces first in the decision process regarding flesh and soul. "However, the spiritual is not first, but the natural, and afterward the spiritual." (1 Corinthians 15:46).

The nearer kinsman, the self or the natural man, had first choice regarding obedience to the law and the purchase of the parcel of land. Boaz represents the second man, who is spiritual and chooses obedience to the ways of God. In the fullness of time, Boaz's opportunity for redemption of the land would come.

Pick of the Crop: Adam represents the first man, that naturally selfish, flesh-driven man of the earth who chose to go against God. The second man is the Lord from heaven with a desire for obedience to the Spirit of God (1 Corinthians 15:47). We've been given the choice in our life to obey our first, natural inclination or to choose to obey the ways of God. Here again the choice is yours.

98 Our Brother's Land

"And I thought to inform you, saying, 'Buy it back in the presence of the inhabitants and the elders of my people. If you will redeem it, redeem it; but if you will not redeem it, then tell me, that I may know; for there is no one but you to redeem it, and I am next after you.'

"And he said, 'I will redeem it.'" Ruth 4:4

Boaz loved Elimelech and sought restitution. They were of the same bone and flesh, though with two completely different passions. This pattern is repeated throughout Scripture for our instruction. Study the lives of the following brothers: Cain and Abel, Ishmael and Isaac, Esau and Jacob, Adam and Jesus. In each case the brothers have two distinct desires: the former and the latter, the first and the second. The first man is flesh or self. The second man is of the spirit with a passion for God. Within all men and women there reside only two paths, to serve the desires of self within your flesh or to serve the desires of the Lord in spirit and in truth.

Both Elimelech and Boaz were faced with decisions in their lives. Elimelech decided to plot a course to Moab, and Boaz worked his fields in Bethlehem. Every big decision is followed by multiple little decisions which culminate into an end result. For Elimelech and his family, his decision was marked by death in Moab, and Boaz alive in Bethlehem wanted to recompense the loss of his brother speedily.

He said, "Buy it back in the presence of the inhabitants and the elders of my people." When Elimelech and his sons died, the family estate fell to the hands of Naomi and Ruth, and the two sought to sell it. In so doing, the purchaser would buy—that is, redeem—the land.

The opportunity for redemption had arrived, and the people of the community had gathered to witness the decision of the near-kinsman. There was a quiet confidence about Boaz, because he knew how the near-kinsman would choose.

Boaz claimed the people for himself, saying they were "my people." There was an innate bond between Boaz and his people. He had a responsibility to do the right thing. He was the type of man who would weep with those who wept and rejoice with those who rejoiced. He was a compassionate man, a caring man. These emotions are not found in self. If we would learn to abandon ourselves for the Savior, we too would embody compassion, caring, and giving for the love of humanity.

"If you will redeem it, redeem it," he said, "but if you will not redeem it, then tell me, that I may know."

There was no partial redemption rule put forth. You were either redeemed or not. The nearest kinsman had the first choice of redemption of land, and Boaz called for his answer.

He said, if this other man did not claim the land, then, "I am next after you." Boaz correctly declared he couldn't make a move until the near-kinsmen had stated his desires. Boaz was a type of the last Adam (Jesus Christ), who was made a living spirit. "And so it is written, 'The first man Adam became a living being.' The last Adam *became* a life-giving spirit" (1 Corinthians 15:45). Christ came after the first Adam, the natural man who is our nearer kinsman. Christ Jesus is God's answer to sin, self, and Satan; and Boaz was the answer for Naomi, Ruth, and their redemption.

"I will redeem it," the man stated. The prospects of accumulating things in this world appealed to the self-life, and he agreed to redeem the land and all the wealth that came with it.

Pick of the Crop: God's redemptive arm reached beyond the salvation of souls. The Promised Land was God's property. Land sold or lost was essentially held captive until redeemed, and God placed redeeming rights in the law (Leviticus 25:23–34). Now Christ has paid the price for the redemption of man and the earth, and Boaz was poised to redeem both Ruth and the land once held by Elimelech, his brother.

99 THE FAILURE OF SELF

"Then Boaz said, 'On the day you buy the field from the hand of Naomi, you must also buy *it* from Ruth the Moabitess, the wife of the dead, to perpetuate the name of the dead through his inheritance.'

"And the close relative said, 'I cannot redeem *it* for myself, lest I ruin my own inheritance. You redeem my right of redemption for yourself, for I cannot redeem *it*.'" Ruth 4:5–6

"Woe to you, scribes and Pharisees, hypocrites! For you pay tithe of mint and anise and cummin, and have neglected the weightier matters of the law: justice and mercy and faith. These you ought to have done, without leaving the others undone" (Matthew 23:23). Self is no better than the Pharisees of our Lord's day, who utilized the law for personal gain and rejected it when souls were in peril. Boaz had skillfully presented Ruth's situation. If someone wanted to redeem the land, he must also redeem Ruth. Furthermore, he must give her children to keep her dead husband's family name alive in Israel.

"I cannot redeem it for myself," the near-kinsman said. Initially, temporal things in the world bring pleasure to our self-will, but when challenged with the redemption of a soul and the resurrection of the name of the dead, self refuses them. "I cannot redeem it for myself."

Beloved, beware of the subtleties of self. There are no redeeming qualities in the self-driven life. The near-kinsman knew of Naomi and Ruth's poverty and plight. He had knowledge of Ruth's piety and refused to obey a law of God. What benefit would he have in offering seed and finance to someone else only to turn over his purchased land to their heirs? The selfish kinsman rejected the idea of saving souls and refused to deliver Ruth. Self cannot see how redemption will benefit him.

He explained, "Lest I ruin my own inheritance." Self is concerned with his image. Pride is first cousin to self-will and is rarely spoken against in Christendom. "These six things the Lord hates, yes, seven are an abomination to Him: A proud look..." (Proverbs 6:16–17). Of the seven things the Lord hates, pride leads the list. Even in the church both pride and the self struggle to stay in the fading spotlight on this world's stage. In many cases you cannot differentiate between entertainment and pulpit.

Self delights in looking good to the eyes of this world. Consider well the time, money, and dialogue you spend on self-help, self-image, and self-esteem vanities. The self-life must die so that we may live.

Pick of the Crop: Humanity fell out of favor with God due to the sin-inspired life that began in the garden. Self will always fail in its pursuit of godliness. Self can never please God, nor can living by the self redeem anyone. "None of them can by any means redeem his brother, nor give to God a ransom for him" (Psalm 49:7). A selfish life is a failed life destined for hell below.

100 THE PLACE OF SELF-RESTRAINT

Listen to our Lord contend with self-will in His humanity.

"For even Christ did not please Himself" (Romans 15:3).

"But made Himself of no reputation, taking the form of a bondservant, and coming in the likeness of men" (Philippians 2:7).

"I can of Myself do nothing. As I hear, I judge; and My judgment is righteous, because I do not seek My own will but the will of the Father who sent Me" (John 5:30).

"For I have not spoken on My own authority; but the Father who sent Me gave Me a command, what I should say and what I should speak" (John 12:49).

"Not My will, but Yours, be done" (Luke 22:42).

In His final hours, they said, "He saved others; Himself He cannot save" (Matthew 27:42), but they could not see Christ taking the sinful selves from all humanity and killing it with His body on that cross. Self must be crucified.

What a contrast in today's society where self is elevated to the highest degree of man's existence.

When the self-life is shackled and properly restrained, you'll find increasing communication with God and decreasing childlike passions. "He must increase, but I *must* decrease" (John 3:30). Your love of others will overcome your love of yourself, and you'll discover a whole new way of living.

Look at the life of a certain centurion, an officer over one hundred soldiers in the Roman army. He was a man of authority, a man of power. He could command any one of his soldiers and servants to go or come, and they would obey. His status in this world offered many reasons for the self-life to take root.

Along his life journey, he had learned that with authority comes responsibility. We're all solely responsible for our own actions. We're all responsible to keep our selfish desires in check, ruling over them. Listen to this man of authority with his foot on the neck of self when he petitions Christ. "I am not worthy that You should enter under my roof. Therefore I did not even think myself worthy to come to You" (Luke 7:6–7). Hear again this man who developed a taste for the temperate lifestyle, "For I also am a man placed under authority, having soldiers under me. And I say to one, 'Go,' and he goes; and to another, 'Come,' and he comes; and to my servant, 'Do this,' and he does *it*" (Luke 7:8).

This centurion had developed a disciplined way of life—true self-control. Imagine a world where men and women ruled their selfish desires. What a difference that would be!

Pick of the Crop: God desires to bring His own family to a place of self-restraint. No longer enslaved by the emotions of our hearts and their strongholds on the body and mind, but rather to live and move with a sound mind, knowing the will of God for our lives and walking therein.

101 The Self Must Yield

"Now this was the custom in former times in Israel concerning redeeming and exchanging, to confirm anything: one man took off his sandal and gave it to the other, and this was a confirmation in Israel. Therefore the close relative said to Boaz, "Buy it for yourself." So he took off his sandal." Ruth 4:7–8

Divorce is a result of the hardening of the heart through selfish desires and a lack of self-control. Self-will is never moved by a committed marriage. Self must move out of the way, relinquishing its will in order for Boaz to complete his work. The same is true with you and me. We must relinquish our will in order for Christ to do His complete work in our hearts and lives. We cannot grow closer to the Bridegroom while in league with self.

The once nearer kinsman thought little of Naomi and Ruth's well-being. Boaz's position was clear. "Behold, I stand at the door and knock. If anyone hears My voice and opens the door, I will come in to him and dine with him, and he with Me." (Revelation 3:20). Christ is a gentleman and will not enter in uninvited. We must open the door to Him. The door of our heart is easily opened when the self moves out of the way. Boaz was eager to commit to marriage, but self-will must first yield.

"So he took off his sandal." There is little labor in removing a sandal, a shoe, an article of clothing, a ring, or even writing a bill of divorce. Contrast that with commitment, patience, perseverance, fostering, laboring, and loving. When this nearer kinsman yielded his will, he would never again have a claim on Naomi and Ruth or their land. He would never again trample their estate underfoot. His sandal had been removed.

Self-will was held in the balance and found wanting. How tragic it is to see others esteem comforts above Christ, their selves above souls, earthly pleasures above heavenly promises. The nearer kinsman's refusal to obey the law of God brought a reproach to him. Instead of securing his own inheritance, his choice heaped humiliation on it. Refusing to save a brother's name marred his own name. The nearer kinsman's name wasn't even written in the Word of God. Your selfish ways will guarantee your name will not be found in the Lamb's Book of Life. By refusing a life of self-denial, you risk being denied by the Crucified Savior.

What is man, in vessels of clay?
At eventide he drifts away.
He boast great things, and fills his stores;
come twilight gloom he is no more.
He curses Christ, despises His day.
By sunset rest, man's in the grave.
And yet,
You touch his flesh. You hold his breath.
Man at best grows less and less.
You made a way.
You brought man in.
It was You who called me friend.
You cleanse my heart; Your blood impart.
A mighty God, O Lord, Thou art.

At judgment call, I was disgraced, a life of sin, a life debase.
You came in haste, stood in my place. No greater love than Your embrace.

Pick of the Crop: We must give up our rights to Christ. In His hand is our hope of redemption. Boaz could not redeem Ruth as long as the nearer kinsmen held on, and your deliverance is not secured, if self refuses to yield its way to Christ.

102 Redemption

"And Boaz said to the elders and all the people, 'You *are* witnesses this day that I have bought all that was Elimelech's, and all that *was* Chilion's and Mahlon's, from the hand of Naomi. Moreover, Ruth the Moabitess, the widow of Mahlon, I have acquired as my wife, to perpetuate the name of the dead through his inheritance, that the name of the dead may not be cut off from among his brethren and from his position at the gate. You *are* witnesses this day.'" Ruth 4:9–10

Naomi and Ruth were in need, and the sale of their land would temporarily deliver them, but they had no future for their family. The purchaser had to agree to terms that included marrying Ruth and bearing children. This could only take place through a kinsman.

Redemption for humanity's blunder into sin's poverty was purchased by the blood of Jesus Christ. Before Christ's death, the blood of animal sacrifices offered a temporary covering of sins. Now, the blood Christ shed is a permanent covering of sin's past, present, and future. Jesus paid the price required by God, and He's espoused to His church, "that he might seek a godly seed" (Malachi 2:15 KJV).

The law said if any stranger came to dwell in Israel, they were not to be mistreated. "The stranger who dwells among you shall be to you as one born among you, and you shall love him as yourself; for you were strangers in the land of Egypt: I am the Lord your God" (Leviticus 19:34). Boaz's love of Ruth stems from his love of the law of God.

Boaz's redeeming rod purchased all the land Elimelech and his sons had owned. He did what Naomi and Ruth could not. If he hadn't rendered recompense, the women, along with their family name, would have perished from Israel, forgotten through fading memories. Likewise, if Christ had not paid the debt this world owed, all humanity would have perished, their families and names forgotten.

He said he would do this "to perpetuate the name of the dead through his inheritance." Elimelech, Chilion and Mahalon were buried with their family name and seed in Moab. But in Bethlehem after Boaz's redemption process their names would be resurrected, appearing again on the pages of Scripture. Boaz could now "perpetuate the name of the dead," that is, resurrect the name of Mahlon. When Elimelech and his sons died, so died their family name. Bethlehem would come to witness this resurrected name in future events.

Pick of the Crop: Boaz paid the price to redeem all that was in jeopardy of being lost. What the nearer kinsman refused to do, Boaz gladly did. All the good intentions of Naomi and Ruth could not redeem or give life to this dead situation. Boaz had prevailed to redeem and raise up children in memory of the dead. Our best efforts to live a life pleasing to God will never work without first being redeemed by Christ. Only then will you begin to see a fruitful life that bears godly, life-giving seed.

103 WITNESSES TO REDEMPTION

Bethlehem witnessed the day of redemption. It was not done in secret. They were there when it happened. All of Bethlehem would come to know this glorious, redemptive love story of Boaz and Ruth. The record would be passed down through Israel's history, Christian teaching, and into eternity.

The Jews witnessed this day. Likewise God's redemption of this world was not done in secret. "Jesus answered him, 'I spoke openly to the world. I always taught in synagogues and in the temple, where the Jews always meet, and in secret I have said nothing'" (John 18:20). The Jews witnessed God's redemptive work. And that work was not limited to the Jews, for God loved the world as well.

The world witnessed this day. At Christ's crucifixion, multitudes had gathered from the major countries of the known world, primarily pilgrims for the feast and festivals. "And there were dwelling in Jerusalem Jews, devout men, from every nation under heaven" (Acts 2:5). Romans reigned in that day and conducted economic trade with men and women from faraway lands. For the world's sake, Pilate hung a title on Christ's cross above His head that read, "JESUS OF NAZARETH, KING OF THE JEWS." "Then many of the Jews read this title, for the place where Jesus was crucified was near the city; and it was written in Hebrew, Greek, and Latin" (John 19:19-20). All who saw that witnessed the event and were without excuse.

Hell witnessed it too. Christ, the Strength of Israel, "having disarmed principalities and powers, He made a public spectacle of them, triumphing over them in it" (Colossians 2:15). All the powers of Hell knew the meaning of this day.

Jerusalem witnessed the resurrected Christ. The two men who had been on the road to Emmaus, were gathered with the disciples and others in Jerusalem to see the resurrected Redeemer. Christ appeared before them and opened their understanding of the Scriptures. "Then He said to them, 'Thus it is written, and thus it was necessary for the Christ to suffer and to rise from the dead the third day, and that repentance and remission of sins should be preached in His name to all nations, beginning at Jerusalem. And you are witnesses of these things." (Luke 24:46–48).

Days later, they told many people what they saw. "And with great power the apostles gave witness to the resurrection of the Lord Jesus. And great grace was upon them all" (Acts 4:33).

Family and friends are witnesses. The death, burial, and resurrected life of Christ is evident in the lives of those who look for His appearing in the clouds with the heavenly angels. A changed life starts from within and pushes outward. A new, redeemed, sanctified life will be noticed by family and friends. It will be undeniable, a witness to those who are lost and a testimony against sin. "Let your light so shine before men, that they may see your good works and glorify your Father in heaven" (Matthew 5:16).

Heaven witnessed Christ's victory. A dark veil was cast across the afternoon sky for about three hours (Mark 15:33). The black sky separated Heaven from Earth, at which time our Lord was forsaken, but not forgotten of the Father. "Yet it pleased the Lord to bruise Him" (Isaiah 53:10). The veil within the temple had separated the Holy of Holies from humanity, God from man, for centuries, but in Christ's victory, both the heavenly veil and the temple veil were torn down (Mark 15:38), opening the way to the Mercy Seat of God, signifying God's acceptance of Christ's offering for sin. Now everyone who believes has equal access to the throne of God.

Christ Himself witnessed it. "And from Jesus Christ, the faithful witness, the firstborn from the dead, and the ruler over the kings of the earth. To Him who loved us and washed us from our sins in His own blood" (Revelation 1:5).

God the Father also witnessed it. "If we receive the witness of men, the witness of God is greater; for this is the witness of God which He has testified of His Son." (1 John 5:9).

Pick of the Crop: God is an equitable God, not willing that any perish. What more could have been done? All creation witnessed His glorious plan of redemption unfolding in Jesus Christ. It was well-documented for our sakes, so rejoice in it and tell others about it.

YOUR THOUGHTS

104 Building of a House

> **"And all the people who were at the gate, and the elders, said, 'We are witnesses. The Lord make the woman who is coming to your house like Rachel and Leah, the two who built the house of Israel; and may you prosper in Ephrathah and be famous in Bethlehem. May your house be like the house of Perez, whom Tamar bore to Judah, because of the offspring which the Lord will give you from this young woman.'" Ruth 4:11–12**

The witnesses pronounced a blessing over the marriage specific to Ruth, likening her womb to Rachel's and Leah's. In other words, may she be fruitful and multiply—a tall order. It recalls another tall order, when God spoke favorably of a great nation, promising Abraham long ago, "I will bless those who bless you, and I will curse him who curses you; and in you all the families of the earth shall be blessed" (Genesis 12:3). Nestled within God's promise was the coming Messiah. Hear again, "For God so loved the world that He gave His only begotten Son, that whoever believes in Him should not perish but have everlasting life" (John 3:16). Both Jew and Gentile are united in God's glorious plan of redemption. Three Gentile women bear witness to this point in Christ's genealogy: Tamar, Rahab and Ruth (Matthew 1:3, 5).

Rachel and Leah were sisters (Genesis 29:16). The two, along with their maids Bilhah and Zilpah, gave birth to the twelve sons and one daughter of Jacob. The names of the children are Reuben, Simeon, Levi, Judah, Dan, Naphtali, Gad, Asher, Issachar, Zebulun, daughter Dinah, Joseph, and Benjamin (Genesis 29:31–35, 30:1–24, 35:16–18).

The sons became fathers, and through the process of time the clan grew to 70 souls (Genesis 46:26–27). A famine forced the entire family to leave the Promise Land and go down into Egypt for 400 years (Genesis 15:13). When the Lord called them out of Egypt, they had grown, numbering about 600,000 men, beside women and children (Exodus 12:37).

But back when they were still a small clan, Tamar, a Gentile, married Er, Judah's oldest son. He died before they could have any children, so Judah told his second son, Onan, to marry Tamar and raise up a son under his brother Er's name. Onan rejected that advice and spilt his seed on the ground in protest. God was displeased, and Onan died.

Judah's third son, Shelah, was too young to be given to Tamar, and Judah, fearful his son might die prematurely, told Tamar to go live with her father until Shelah grew up. Judah never intended to let his youngest son marry Tamar.

Time passed. After the death of Judah's wife, he went to the city of Timnah to shear sheep. Knowing this, Tamar dressed herself in the attire of a prostitute, covered her face, and sat by the side of the road on the way to Timnah. When Judah saw her, unaware she was his daughter-in-law, he agreed to lie with her and pay her with a young goat of his flock at a later date. In the interim he gave her his bracelet and staff as a guarantee of his word.

After he left, Tamar returned home without telling anyone what she had done. Judah sent a young goat to pay the prostitute, but no one knew the woman of whom he spoke. Three months passed, and people told Judah that Tamar had become pregnant by prostitution. Judah threatened to burn her to death, but Tamar brought out the articles of security, saying, "By the man to whom these belong, I *am* with child." Judah recognized his pledged goods and repented of his sin. Tamar gave birth to twin boys, Perez and Zarah (Genesis 38).

Tamar, clever in conception, sought what was rightfully hers. She understood the importance of marriage and the value of the seed of God's people. Judah testified to this, saying, "She has been more righteous than I, because I did not give her to Shelah my son" (Genesis 38:26).

The people of Bethlehem said, "May your house be like the house of Perez, whom Tamar bore to Judah." Few words are recorded regarding the life and times of Perez. He is mentioned among the sons of Judah and that he had two sons of his own, Hezron and Hamul (Genesis 46:12). Perez obtained the position of Judah's second-born son after Er and Onan's death (Numbers 26:20). It's suggested his descendants were numerous, and the people hope for the same fruitfulness from Ruth's womb. Distant relatives of Perez became notable, mighty men who initiated the service of King David in the first month of the year. Twenty four thousand men of war are recorded, not to mention their families, women and children (1 Chronicles 27:1–3).

So Tamar, Ruth, and Ruth's new mother-in-law, Rahab of Jericho, were all Gentiles married into the Jewish nation, and the people of Bethlehem hoped they would be blessed, "because of the offspring which the Lord will give you from this young woman."

The promise of God is disclosed here in the word *offspring* or *seed*. "For verily he took not on him the nature of angels; but he took on him the seed of Abraham" (Hebrews 2:16 KJV). The seed which the Lord shall give Ruth will germinate, culminating into Jesus Christ, just as Mary was told "that Holy One who is to be born will be called the Son of God" (Luke 1:35). Yes, Naomi and Ruth, the child who would come to you is a type of redeemer. Better still, someone greater than he will come, who will be famous in Ephrathah and Bethlehem.

Pick of the Crop: The family of our Lord had humble beginnings in this earth, but inherited a great house. Not simply a place to dwell, rather it's a house built of godly descendants, a special pedigree born of the seed of the woman. You, lover of God, have a gloriously wonderful future awaiting.

105 Law, Labor, Marriage, Family

"So Boaz took Ruth and she became his wife; and when he went in to her, the Lord gave her conception, and she bore a son." Ruth 4:13

Four branches of God's government were given to this world: Law, Labor, Marriage, and Family.

Law: God gave His rule of conduct, His law, outlining man's responsibility of obedience for the good of mankind. "And the Lord God commanded the man, saying, 'Of every tree of the garden you may freely eat; but of the tree of the knowledge of good and evil you shall not eat, for in the day that you eat of it you shall surely die'" (Genesis 2:16–17).

Labor: God gave man employment for his pleasures. "Then the Lord God took the man and put him in the garden of Eden to tend and keep it" (Genesis 2:15). A nonproductive man is an unhappy man, because he has nothing to live for.

Marriage: God said it was not good for man to be alone, so God created the woman from the man and brought her to the man. God gave marriage, the joining together of man and woman for the pleasures of each other's presence and to partake of the fruit of their labors.

And Adam said:

"This *is* now bone of my bones
And flesh of my flesh;
She shall be called Woman,
Because she was taken out of Man."

> Therefore a man shall leave his father and mother and be joined to his wife, and they shall become one flesh. And they were both naked, the man and his wife, and were not ashamed. (Genesis 2:23–25)

Family: God gave the man and the woman the ability to procreate and build a family for a united fellowship, fruitfulness, and fullness in the service of God, to rule over His creation. "Then God blessed them, and God said to them, 'Be fruitful and multiply; fill the earth and subdue it; have dominion over the fish of the sea, over the birds of the air, and over every living thing that moves on the earth'" (Genesis 1:28).

All the above are witnessed by the world. When obeyed they help build social order, but if anyone of these pillars are omitted, disorder ensues. By toppling these pillars you'll topple a nation.

Boaz obeyed the law regarding kinsmen, was employed and an employer, and married Ruth to begin their family. "Prepare your outside work, make it fit for yourself in the field; and afterward build your house" (Proverbs 24:27). Their family will prosper because the law of God promotes the prosperity of those who obey Him. Contrast these principles with the way this current culture flows, and you'll begin to understand why disorder and unemployment are up. Opponents of marriage have risen, divorce is popular, abortion is on the rise, and the family is faltering.

Pick of the Crop: Honorable marriages are luminous lights in this spiritually dark world, a high calling of heaven among the low standards of humanity. Parents, walk worthy of the call to instruct your children in the way of holy living, pleasing to God, and in due season, they will instruct their children to the glory of God.

106 Taken and Loved

"So Boaz took Ruth and she became his wife." Ruth 4:13

Can the depth of love be searched, whose fountain freely flows?

Think back to where you were, physically, mentally, and spiritually when the Lord found you. It was a dark, lonely time, wasn't it? You thought everything was all right, when in reality it wasn't. Now reflect on your journey, the ups and downs, ebbs and flows. They were all under Christ's leading, carrying you into the Promised Land of God. What a wonderful journey! As Boaz took Ruth to be his wife, so too Christ has taken us.

> Or do you not know, brethren (for I speak to those who know the law), that the law has dominion over a man as long as he lives? For the woman who has a husband is bound by the law to her husband as long as he lives. But if the husband dies, she is released from the law of her husband. So then if, while her husband lives, she marries another man, she will be called an adulteress; but if her husband dies, she is free from that law, so that she is no adulteress, though she has married another man. Therefore, my brethren, you also have become dead to the law through the body of Christ, that you may be married to another—to Him who was raised from the dead, that we should bear fruit to God. For when we were in the flesh, the sinful passions which were aroused by the law were at work in our members to bear fruit to death. But now we have been delivered from the law, having died to what we

> were held by, so that we should serve in the newness of the Spirit and not in the oldness of the letter. (Romans 7:1–6)

All that Boaz has Ruth has: his field, his fame, his fortune, and his family forever. Likewise, we who are called of God have divorced our lifestyle of sin and have married Christ Jesus. He is rich in wisdom, knowledge, and judgment. All that He has we have: His Father, His family, His Life, His legacy, and His love.

His banner over me,
as far as eye can see,
with beauty wondrously,
is love.

Pick of the Crop: No one can love you as Christ Jesus can. We were taken out of sin and blessed with a love the land of Moab cannot offer. We were married into the everlasting family of God. Anyone else's love (spouse, family member, stranger or friend) is limited and will cease at their death, but the love of Christ is an everlasting love.

107 The Fruitful Life

The Lord says He gave her conception. Ruth's marvelously wonderful journey carried her from widow in Moab to wife in Bethlehem to a mother in Israel. "Many, O Lord my God, are Your wonderful works which You have done; and Your thoughts toward us cannot be recounted to You in order; if I would declare and speak of them, they are more than can be numbered" (Psalm 40:5).

"And as Isaiah said before: 'Unless the Lord of Sabaoth had left us a seed, we would have become like Sodom, and we would have been made like Gomorrah" (Romans 9:29). Boaz and Ruth lived during the days when the judges ruled, and although the nation as a whole was laden with sins and iniquities, God kept it from complete annihilation. He made an example of the cities of Sodom and Gomorrah, which were consumed by sinful lifestyles (Genesis 19:24–25 and 2 Peter 2:6). There were a few in Israel who sought the leading of God in their lives, and for those few as well as the promise made to Abraham, God kept His royal seed alive in the midst of darkness, sustaining a remnant from the masses.

As in the days of Boaz and Ruth, so today there is a very small remnant of men and women who love God. For those few, His seed has born life within their souls: "having been born again, not of corruptible seed but incorruptible, through the word of God which lives and abides forever" (1 Peter 1:23). For those who long after His counseling, correction, and direction, His seed will produce seed after its own kind. When God brings us to Himself, we're joined in a divine union to Him. In such a relationship, should we expect anything less than holy conception?

Life in Christ is a fruitful life where His seed is born again into the lives of the few. "For many are called, but few are chosen" (Matthew 22:14).

When Christ is conceived, His seed is born into a soul. This seed produces fruit, as we see in the life of our sister Ruth. Glance back to her former life as someone married in the world of Moab. There's no evidence of fruit, her womb was barren, and the same can be said of her sister-in-law. Why? They were "dead in trespasses and sins" (Ephesians 2:1). Once brought into Bethlehem, Ruth was married to the giver of life who passed onto her that seed which the Lord has blessed. Notice the divine order that's different from the world: marriage, consummation, conception, and child. Unto Ruth a child is born; unto Ruth a son is given. The prophecy of the witnesses within the gate has been fulfilled.

Pick of the Crop: We are expected to bear fruit in this life (John 15:16), manifested in an ever-growing love of God, a desire to serve God in good works, praying, and fasting (to name a few). As in the natural realm, fruit honors God and man (Judges 9:9). Can this be said of you? Ask God to help us be the bearer of spiritual fruit in this world.

108 For His Purposes

God puts marriages together primarily for His purposes and not solely for our pleasures. He wants to mold and shape us into the image of His Son, and for many, marriage will facilitate this process.

Ruth would learn to release her will to Boaz, and he would release his to Ruth. A major milestone never reached in many marriages is the releasing of wills. Why is this so difficult? One reason is a lack of trust. We fear the pain that will come from submitting to someone else. But God's plan for marriage is to make the two become one. "Therefore a man shall leave his father and mother and be joined to his wife, and they shall become one flesh" (Genesis 2:24).

However, when the two that are joined together never fully release their wills to each other, they will continually pull apart. Husband and wife are individuals with their own personalities, roles, and needs, which are not to be taken lightly, but thinking and living as one flesh with one desire to please God in marriage should be their mutual goal.

Another tool God uses to mold married couples to His will is the caring and rearing of children. A beautiful baby needs food, water, clothing, sheltering, loving, touching, caressing, and communicating. As a child grows, so does their personality, requiring training, understanding, and discipline from both parents. As parents, we assist our little ones with their battles against self-will. If you allow it, a child's presence in your home will cut away at your loosely held wants or passions and replace them with their own needs. Our priority changes, our sleep pattern changes, our will changes to not my will but the child's will be done within reason. Our caring, giving, and loving focuses on ministering and serving this little person.

The pattern of serving can be viewed in part as God's care for you and me, and we in turn ought to transfer this model of giving to our child and to our spouse. The more we learn to love and trust our spouse, the more Christ's character is formed in us. Marriage can be viewed as a lifestyle of releasing your will, not of taking but giving.

Marriage sealed between two souls,
Time reveals Christ's work unfolds.

A cutting away of both flesh,
The Lord knows what is best.

The image of Him, God's beloved Son.
He'll shape and mold till the two become one.

Boaz's first meeting with Ruth was sweetly glazed with a giving character. He gave her employment, advice, direction, and protection. He offered water for her thirst. He spoke a blessing over her, fed her, and gave her a special place at his table. He gave her a special position alongside of the reapers. He gave her special handfuls of barley, purposefully left for her to glean, and a gift to be carried to Naomi. He covered her, encouraged her, promised her, and loved her.

Ruth's first meeting with Boaz came after giving up her life in Moab. She gave herself in service to Naomi and the people of Israel. She gave her testimony and her time. She honored Boaz, gave him good work, and gave him herself.

Pick of the Crop: We're all a work in progress to God for his glory and honor. Whatever your lot in life, exercise it for the love of God. Now that you are joined to Christ, everything you have—your marriage, job, and pleasures—is for God's greater purpose, which at times may be beyond your and my plans.

109 Never Give Up Hope

"Then the women said to Naomi, 'Blessed be the Lord, who has not left you this day without a close relative; and may his name be famous in Israel! And may he be to you a restorer of life and a nourisher of your old age; for your daughter-in-law, who loves you, who is better to you than seven sons, has borne him.'" Ruth 4:14–15

The women, likely those who met Naomi after she returned from Moab with a sulky spirit, celebrated with her. They praised and blessed the Lord over the birth of the kinsman child. So, too, the heavenly host praised God at the birth of the other kinsman child, King Jesus (Luke 2:13–14).

The fame of this lovely little lad was preceded by the fame of his parents and grandmother and the work God did within their lives. Three prophecies regarding the child are before us, but they point more specifically to Christ.

1. "His name may be famous in Israel." There's no other name under heaven that can evoke both praise and contempt among mortals than the name of Jesus Christ.

Jesus means Savior. "And you shall call His name Jesus, for He will save His people from their sins" (Matthew 1:21).

Jesus literally embodies salvation. "Nor is there salvation in any other, for there is no other name under heaven given among men by which we must be saved" (Acts 4:12).

All the Old Testament prophets testified about the salvation through His name. Every prophet of God from Abel to John the Baptist spoke of the saving name of Jesus. "To Him all the prophets witness that, through His name, whoever believes in Him will receive remission of sins" (Acts 10:43).

Furthermore, the Scripture says, "He will be great and will be called the Son of the Highest" (Luke 1:32). The greatest man to have ever lived and died and rose again is none other than Jesus the Christ.

2. "A restorer of life." We've seen Naomi's voyage from a wife and mother, to a widow and mourner. Praise be to God, He was not finished with her. She had become a grandmother. Hallelujah! What had been impossible was now a reality. Naomi's life had been restored. Her family name had been born again, and now she lived vicariously through her grandson.

Dear friend, never give up hope in God. We're told, "When my father and my mother forsake me, then the Lord will take care of me" (Psalm 27:10). God is a God of the impossible. Trust Him to come through for you in ways past finding out. Christ Jesus is the restorer of life to the dead and the lost.

That holy thing was heaven sent to those
who weep and long lament.
To comfort all that mourn and cry,
anguish of soul and sorrow sigh.

He helps the grieved, their sins relieved.
In misery he heard their plea.
That holy thing has filled my heart with
love and joy from him impart.

3. "A nourisher of your old age." We must learn to trust God in our latter days, because only God can feed, provide, sustain, and guide. God's promise for the latter years is this, "Even to your old age, I am He, and even to gray hairs I will carry you! I have made, and I will bear; even I will carry, and will deliver you" (Isaiah 46:4).

A spouse may die, friends pass on, and children move away. All others may forget us, but not God. There's service to be found in God in our latter days.

We find Abraham serving God at seventy-five years old (Genesis 12:4), and at eighty-six years of age (Genesis 16:16). We see him again at ninety-nine years old (Genesis 17:1) and at one hundred, his wife Sarah being ninety, both found in the service God (Genesis 17:17).

Sarah reached the age of 127 (Genesis 23:1). Abraham's recorded death was at 175 years old (Genesis 25:7). Both experienced rich, full lives under God guidance. God did not cast them off when they were old, but nurtured and nourished them along the way.

Job lived 140 years after his afflictions and the trying of his faith in the service of the Lord (Job 42:16).

In the temple, Anna the prophetess was eighty-four years old, and we're told she "served God with fastings and prayers night and day" (Luke 2:37). In her faithful service to God, she saw Jesus.

Dear saints, God offers many ways to serve Him in the latter years of life. Ask the Lord to show you, because in true service, you reveal Jesus and God will reveal Jesus to you in the Word.

In Anna's faithful service, Christ was revealed, "And coming in that instant she gave thanks to the Lord, and spoke of Him to all those who looked for redemption in Jerusalem" (Luke 2:38). Abraham served God as an old man, and Christ was revealed to him. Jesus testified of it, "Your father Abraham rejoiced to see My day, and he saw it and was glad" (John 8:56). Naomi found her place to serve in the latter days in connection to her grandson.

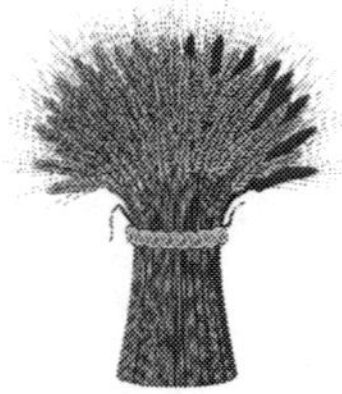

Pick of the Crop: God loves and honors the elderly in ways the world does not know. We have fallen a great distance from the time when the young would stand and give honor in the presence of the grey-headed senior (Leviticus 19:32). Grey hair is a crown of glory if righteousness is found to reside therein (Proverbs 16:31). Your course is nearly complete. The final touches on your purification will end, but until then there's work to do. Embrace a child, encourage a friend, and impart wisdom all in the service of the God who has not forsaken you.

110 Active Love

"For your daughter-in-law, who loves you . . ." The women went on to say Naomi's daughter-in-law loved her, not merely superficially, but a deep, heart-felt love demonstrated in words and deeds. This lane on love's endless highway leads to love's active side seen in the spirit of serving. Ruth went to Bethlehem, not to be served, but to serve.

"Who is better to you than seven sons." The women exalted Ruth above the ranks of seven sons. Elkanah, the husband of Hannah, mother of Samuel the prophet, asked, "Am I not better to you than ten sons?" (1 Samuel 1:8). But all the world's sons and daughters could never do what the Sun of Righteousness has done.

> But to you who fear My name
> The Sun of Righteousness shall arise
> With healing in His wings;
> And you shall go out
> And grow fat like stall-fed calves. (Malachi 4:2)

Love awakes a weary mother to comfort a restless child in the night. Love labors while others lounge. Love lifts while scorners lampoon. Love loosens while haters limit. Love lives and the world suffers loss. Love will ultimately correct all wrong.

Love is the greatest heralding peace,
When prophecy fails and tongues cease.
Though I do all to feed the poor,
Love is the greater; love implores.

All mysteries and knowledge will be in vain
Without love to sustain.
Covet the best, a more excellent way.
Love is the greatest; love will remain.

Pick of the Crop: Love is best demonstrated in action: the love of God gave (John 3:16), the love of God died (1 John 3:16), the love of Jacob served (Genesis 29:20, 30). Your love of God will cause you to observe His commands (John 14:15), and your love of the believers will cause you to honor them (Romans 12:10).

111 Nestled at Her Bosom

"Then Naomi took the child and laid him on her bosom, and became a nurse to him. Also the neighbor women gave him a name, saying, 'There is a son born to Naomi.' And they called his name Obed. He is the father of Jesse, the father of David." Ruth 4:16–17

In Moab, Naomi laid her husband and sons in the cold bowels of the earth. In Bethlehem, Naomi laid her grandson in the warmth of her bosom.

The bosom is the center of an intimate, affectionate union with Jehovah. The bosom is where your every breath is heard and where the sensations of the heart are understood. The weight of the ones you love is borne upon the bosom of the heart and carried before the Lord, as did Aaron, the High Priest of God. He carried the names of the twelve tribes of Israel upon his heart in the form of a breastplate. "So Aaron shall bear the names of the sons of Israel on the breastplate of judgment over his heart, when he goes into the holy place, as a memorial before the Lord continually" (Exodus 28:29).

The disciple whom our Lord loved, who drank richly of the Divine, was seen leaning upon the bosom of Christ. "Now there was leaning on Jesus' bosom one of His disciples, whom Jesus loved" (John 13:23).

The young, love-sick Shulamite in the absence of her lover declared him to be as a sweet smelling bundle of perfume lying between her breasts at night. "A bundle of myrrh is my beloved to me, that lies all night between my breasts" (Song of Solomon 1:13). We are in a deep, safe, contemplative state of endless love when we are found in the bosom of the Father. Has the Spirit of God placed someone upon your heart? Bear them before the Father. "The only begotten Son, who is in the bosom of the Father, He has declared Him" (John 1:18).

Imagine the joy this child brought into the bosom of the world of Naomi, Ruth, and Boaz. His first cries, his first smile. They experienced his first words, his first steps. They taught him the oracles of the Almighty, and he grew to become famous in Israel.

Pick of the Crop: What is the dearest desire laid upon your heart thus far in your journey? Is it the joy of the Lord or the delights of your family? For Naomi, her bitterness was replaced with the sweet pleasures of her first grandchild. Nestled in the center of our affections ought to be God and His goodness toward us. Just as Naomi did not find it in Moab, we will not reach this state living outside God's will.

112 Renewed Life

The testimony of the women is very significant, "There is a son born to Naomi." They understood the severe loss of life Naomi suffered while away from Bethlehem. The women knew the importance of family, a kinsman, and inheritance. The women perceived the hand of God orchestrating this death-transforming-life experience.

The beauty of the women's devoted love for Naomi is evident in their testimony, attributing the birth of the child to Naomi. Her labor and anguish, sufferings and pains within the depths of her soul, coupled with a renewed hope in Jehovah-jireh (YHWH, Yahweh will provide) has delivered this child.

Naomi travailed in spirit over the birth of this child similar to the apostle Paul's travail over the souls of those he ministered to. "My little children, for whom I labor in birth again until Christ is formed in you" (Galatians 4:19). Both labored as spiritual parents suffering the spiritual contractions as if they were with child, pushing toward the birth and subsequent rest. A family name was resurrected in Israel. Here again in the eyes of Naomi, that which had been dead was now alive, that which had been lost was now found.

"And they called his name Obed. He is the father of Jesse, the father of David."

Their neighbors affectionately named the child Obed, which means *service*. Trusting the child will pattern his life after the life of his mother, who faithfully served Boaz, Naomi, and the people of Israel.

The dark mysterious path of the divine seed is revealed through this marriage. Obed grew, and in the course of time he had a son named Jesse. Jesse had a son named David, and we see the delightful pedigree of Obed, who fathered Jesse, who fathered David, King of Israel. The wonders of God! A more robust genealogy is given to us in the verses that follow.

Pick of the Crop: Consider again how Naomi's womb had been closed, and yet a child was born to her. You were once dead and have been born again to new life in Christ. God took our nonviable life and has born to Himself sons and daughters, an implausible miracle made manifest in mankind. Hallelujah!

113 The Genealogy: Enclosed by God

"Now this *is* the genealogy of Perez: Perez begot Hezron; Hezron begot Ram, and Ram begot Amminadab; Amminadab begot Nahshon, and Nahshon begot Salmon; Salmon begot Boaz, and Boaz begot Obed; Obed begot Jesse, and Jesse begot David." Ruth 4:18–22

Perez means a *breach*. A child born of an irreparable act was placed in the line of the Messiah. This speaks of the mercies of God toward humanity.

Sin struck a breach, crafting a gap between mankind and God. Perez's parents placed him in this predicament. The same is true with you and me. The breach before us can be traced back to our parents and further back to the Garden of Eden, where the breach of sin entered in, separating the world from God. All have sinned, coming short of God's glory, but through belief in the name of Christ Jesus, we are part of the family of the Messiah.

Perez had a son named Hezron. *Hezron* means *surrounded* or *enclosed*. He was with the family of Israel when they went to dwell in Egypt (Genesis 46:12). His name speaks of God providing His protective barrier to us while we live in this world surrounded by the sin of the world. Satan himself acknowledges this barrier while contending for Job. "Have You not made a hedge around him, around his household, and around all that he has on every side? You have blessed the work of his hands, and his possessions have increased in the land" (Job 1:10).

God has surrounded you and all that you have: health, wealth, family, and reputation. His protective love watches over and surrounds those who will remain under Him, as a hen covers her brood. As an added blessing, "the angel of the Lord encamps all around those who fear Him, and delivers them" (Psalm 34:7). The only time Satan can harm anything dear to us is by God's permission. He cannot act without God's approval. "And the Lord said to Satan, 'Behold, all that he has is in your power; only do not lay a hand on his person'" (Job 1:12). For Christ Jesus, God surrounded Him and protected Him until His hour had come.

A time will come when our spiritual and physical faculties will be assaulted. Remember the Word of our Lord: "Fear not, for I am with you; be not dismayed, for I am your God. I will strengthen you, yes, I will help you, I will uphold you with My righteous right hand" (Isaiah 41:10). The Lord will allow the difficult times; nevertheless, His love continues to surround. Satan desires to sift us like wheat, but when he's finished, we can strengthen those around us. God allowed Satan to sift Naomi for a season in order to produce the seed she longed for.

Pick of the Crop: The family of God is like an enclosed garden, a city surrounded by a wall. Nothing can enter in without the knowledge and will of our Lord. We are literally enclosed with Emmanuel's enforcements. His protection offers assurance through this life.

114 The Genealogy: Living Above Circumstances

Surrounded by God while in the midst of the world, Hezron had a son named Ram. *Ram* means *high*. He is believed to have been born down in Egypt due to the omission of his name from the genealogy of the tribe of Judah prior to their entering Egypt.

Ram's name first appears in the account of Ruth, and he is mentioned later in a genealogy of Judah (1 Chronicles 2:9–10). Living in Egypt with a name like Ram can teach us the importance of living above our circumstances and keeping our affections on heavenly things. As children of the Divine, we should live high above the base things of this current age, things that hold the lovers of this world down, preventing them from mounting up on high.

The sins of Egypt reached high into Pharaoh's palace. As with the sins of this age, no nation, government, or ruler is immune. Don't take sin lightly. It always attempts to hold down the righteous. The sins at the top germinate down to local legislation, "I have seen the wicked in great power, and spreading himself like a native green tree" (Psalm 37:35). Sin overshadowed the righteous in Egypt and in this current age, but the Lord sees it all. "The eyes of the Lord are in every place, keeping watch on the evil and the good" (Proverbs 15:3).

Noah and his family were lifted high above the earth in a deluge (Genesis 7:17). Daniel was raised up from the lions' den (Daniel 6:23), and Paul and Silas prayed and sang in prison, lifting up their voices to God (Acts 16:25). All these focused on God and not their current circumstances.

The Bible list four creatures that are little on this earth but are wise in their thinking. Their situation, circumstances, or lack of substance does not prevent them from succeeding (Proverbs 30:24-28).

The ant is not strong in the way we humans understand strength. They have no way of producing food, but in the summer they perceive the season of opportunity and go out gathering in anticipation for the coming winter. The child of God should learn to be wise and to recognize the seasons of opportunities, taking full advantage of the time God has provided.

The conies (rock badgers) are known as a "feeble folk," but do not let their feeble strength and character prevent them from overcoming adversities. In their wisdom they build their homes in the rocks. Likewise, we should be able to look upon these creatures and receive instructions. When we're weak and faint in the way, we do what the feeble folk do, making homes within the cleft of the rock where God shelters (Exodus 33:22).

The locust have no king and are easily disbursed, trampled by the foot of man. But they know there's strength in numbers. The Messiah does not raise mavericks for the ministry. We are not to forsake the gathering together with other believers as some have done (Hebrews 10:25). We unlike the locust have a king to lead us collectively in the way we should go.

The spider—some interpret this as being a lizard—has limited defenses, except for the fact that they can be found living among the kings of the world. This should be our state of mind. Christians are easily outnumbered by the trappings of this sinful age, but if we make our home within the secret tabernacle of the Most High God, we'll find the protection of the king's palace.

Pick of the Crop: The family of God are to support one another, to encourage those in the body who need our help. Those who are born of God have overcome the world, and it is our faith in God that gives us the victory (1 John 5:4). In a strong family, we can piece life circumstances together into a collective work of God, assembling rocky times and rough relations into a lovely vessel of honor, sanctified and fit for the Master's use.

115 The Genealogy: Christ, Our Kinsman

Ram had a son named Amminadab, whose beautiful name means *my kinsman willing*. His name directs us to the heart of Christ, our kinsman, who willingly gave Himself as a sacrifice for the sins of the world.

> Therefore, when He came into the world, He said:
> "Sacrifice and offering You did not desire,
> But a body You have prepared for Me.
> In burnt offerings and sacrifices for sin
> You had no pleasure.
> Then I said, 'Behold, I have come—
> In the volume of the book it is written of Me—
> To do Your will, O God.'"
>
> Previously saying, "Sacrifice and offering, burnt offerings, and offerings for sin You did not desire, nor had pleasure in them" (which are offered according to the law), then He said, "Behold, I have come to do Your will, O God." He takes away the first that He may establish the second. By that will we have been sanctified through the offering of the body of Jesus Christ once for all.
>
> And every priest stands ministering daily and offering repeatedly the same sacrifices, which can never take away sins. But this Man, after He had offered one sacrifice for sins forever, sat down at the right hand of God. (Hebrews 10:5–12)

Animal sacrifices and burnt offerings could not eternally remove sin from our hearts. Jesus gave Himself without measure, exactly as the Scriptures foretold He would. We're related to Christ; He's our kinsman. The god-gene resides within the people of God. We are born of God, bathed in the blood line of Christ. When Christ becomes your kinsman you are part of an eternal family legacy made up of both Old and New Testament saints of God.

Are you experiencing difficulties at this time in your walk? Read the writings of our brother King David within the Psalms and be encouraged. Are you needing courage to take a stand for righteousness? Read the account of the life of our sister Queen Esther and be strengthened. Are you needing to learn a life of discipline before the Lord, staying focused on Him and not distracted by the cares of this world? Study the life of two of our sisters Mary and Martha of Bethany (Luke 10:38-42).

The Word is filled with practical lessons passed down from believers, like you and I, who have the Spirit of Jesus Christ, our kinsman, dwelling in us to do great work.

Amminadab was the father-in-law of Aaron the High Priest through the marriage of his daughter, Elisheba (Exodus 6:23).

Pick of the Crop: For the family of God, Christ Jesus is our kinsman. He is our avenger, provider, deliver, and savior, who rescues the needy out of all their distress. He knows your name and has called you friend (John 15:15).

116 The Genealogy: Born to Greatness

Amminadab had a son named Nahshon. *Nahshon* means *enchanter*. His name implies he had a godly gift beyond normal human possession. He was a great man, and he points to Jesus, the greatest of men.

Nahshon was a prince in Judah, chosen to assist Moses in ministering to the people of God (Numbers 1:7, 16). Jesus is the Prince of Peace (Isaiah 9:6), the Lion of the Tribe of Judah (Revelation 5:5). Jesus fashioned His ministry for all mankind.

Nahshon was captain over 74,600 fighting men of the tribe of Judah, and he pitched his tent facing east toward the rising of the sun (Numbers 2:3–4). Jesus is the Captain of our salvation (Hebrews 2:10), the Captain of the army of the Lord (Joshua 5:13–14). He will return to earth out of the eastern sky (Matthew 24:27).

Nahshon was the first prince to make an offering to God (Numbers 7:12). "How much more shall the blood of Christ, who through the eternal Spirit offered Himself without spot to God, cleanse your conscience from dead works to serve the living God?" (Hebrews 9:14). Nahshon was the grandfather of Boaz.

Consider another great man named Melchizedek, which means, king of righteousness. He was the king of Salem, which means peace. He had no father nor mother, no genealogy, no beginning nor end. He's like the Son of God, a priest forever, to whom Abraham gave tithe (Hebrews 7:1–4). Now consider this, Jesus was made a high priest of God forever after the order of Melchizedek (Hebrews 6:20).

Pick of the Crop: The family of God through His power will do valiantly (Psalm 60:12), and the people that know their God shall be strong and do exploits (Daniel 11:32). There are great possibilities awaiting those who love the name of our Lord. Our great high priest is before the throne of God interceding for you and me right now. He's watching and waiting to answer our needs.

117 The Genealogy: Our Covering

Nahshon had a son named Salmon. *Salmon* means *covering*. He became a covering for Rahab's former way of life.

Our old life of sin requires an atonement, which Christ Jesus accomplished. "Therefore, in all things He had to be made like His brethren, that He might be a merciful and faithful High Priest in things pertaining to God, to make propitiation for the sins of the people" (Hebrews 2:17).

Rahab's lifestyle of prostitution was no different from our spiritual life of prostitution when we were separated from Christ. We all ran headstrong toward the gratification of our sensations, following any traveling spirit that knocked at the door of our inordinate desires. We opened our souls to any filthy spirit wishing to ravish us, yielding our wills to them with little care for what they may do.

The Gentiles also multiplied their harlotries, living in the moment. We were born naked into this world, spiritually fondled by our sinful passions, being pimped from pillar to post (Ezekiel 23:19–21). "At that time you were without Christ, being aliens from the commonwealth of Israel and strangers from the covenants of promise, having no hope and without God in the world. But now in Christ Jesus you who once were far off have been brought near by the blood of Christ" (Ephesians 2:12–13). The power of Jesus' blood has a spiritual effect that's not restricted to physical space or time restraints as we know it. His blood is ubiquitous, covering sins of the past, present, and future.

Rahab the harlot had been lost, and the love of God found her in the world. She had run toward pleasures, and God gave her His promises. The harlot had sought out men, but the Heavenly gave her a husband.

Rahab believed the Word of God, and God blessed her with Salmon as her covering. Salmon and Rahab are the parents of Boaz (Matthew 1:5).

Pick of the Crop: It's a cold night outside the gates of the palace. A leper lies naked with putrefied sores. Now imagine the son of the king of that palace coming out at his father's command, calling the leper by name and covering him with his royal robe, cleaning him up, and inviting him into his palace. That leper was you and I, and the son was Jesus. Having entered His palace, we are in His family, covered in His righteousness.

118 The Genealogy: Swift Strength

Boaz means *fleeting* or *swiftly.* Recall how swift Boaz was to encourage Ruth to remain in his field and how alert he was to attend to her at meal time? He did not delay seating Ruth next to his reapers. He was quick to instruct his servants to leave extra crops for Ruth to gather. He hastened his hands to give grain to Ruth and Naomi. He quickly covered Ruth with his garment. He rushed to take a stand for Ruth in the court of justice before the elders of the people of Israel. He accelerated exposing of the heart of the nearest kinsman. Boaz raced to redeem Ruth.

Boaz's name appears on one of the two pillars King Solomon sanctioned to stand before the temple of the Lord (2 Chronicles 3:17). The pillar bearing Boaz's name is a picture of Christ's swift strength. Christ Jesus standing before the temple of our heart gives us strength, leading His people through the world by day and by night.

Our lovely Lord is mighty and swift. He comes leaping upon the mountains of our adversities, skipping up on the hills of our sorrows. Christ is like a glorious gallant gazelle (Song of Solomon 2:8-9), no summit is beyond His reach.

"I will lift up mine eyes unto the hills, from whence cometh my help. My help *comes* from the Lord, who made heaven and earth" (Psalm 121:1-2).

Boaz became Ruth's priest, protector, provider, pillar, passion, praise, and purchaser. Their son was named Obed.

Pick of the Crop: "*The righteous* cry out, and the Lord hears, and delivers them out of all their troubles" (Psalm 34:17). Cry out to God in time of trouble and don't rely on man. Call out to God now. God in all His strength will come and deliver you.

119 The Genealogy: A Life of Service

Obed means *to serve.* He lived a life of service that was not included in Scripture as a lesson to us. Self will seek its own glory in almost everything, even the service of God.

Obed's presence restored life to his grandmother, nourishing her latter days. The details are excluded, yet here again, the Word of the Lord is true—Obed was famous in Israel. He led a secret life of service, giving his life for the glory of God, and was rewarded openly. Obed's name appears in the genealogies of Christ (Matthew 1:5, Luke 3:32).

Our works are watched and motives weighed.
No service for Christ will go unpaid.

Obed is the grandfather of King David. His son was Jesse, which means *to exist.* Jesse fashioned his life out of the service he learned from his father, Obed. Jesse's existence to serve was an example to his family, the nation of Israel, and lovers of God in today's world. When there was a matter with the King, the kingdom, or the people, Jesse's acts of service came in giving.

His existence was encompassed by a lifestyle of giving. He gave his three eldest sons to serve in King Saul's army (1 Samuel 17:13). He gave gifts to his eldest sons and to their captain, carried by the hands of his youngest son (1 Samuel 17:17–18). He gave his son David to the service of King Saul and the nation of Israel. David became the king's personal armor-bearer and musician (1 Samuel 16:21–23).

For the love of giving as a service to God, "Jesse took a donkey loaded with bread, a skin of wine, and a young goat and sent them by his son

David to Saul" (1 Samuel 16:20). The prophet Zechariah wrote about an event like this, looking toward the day of our Lord: "Rejoice greatly, O daughter of Zion! Shout, O daughter of Jerusalem! Behold, your King is coming to you; He is just and having salvation, Lowly and riding on a donkey, A colt, the foal of a donkey" (Zechariah 9:9). With the bread, the wine, and the sacrifice (goat), this gift looked forward to the perfect gift of the Messiah.

The carpenter's son would one day ride into Jerusalem on a donkey sent by His Eternal Father (Matthew 13:55; John 12:12–14). He is the rod growing from the stem of Jesse, bearing fruit (Isaiah 11:1). He is the Bread of Life who shed His blood as a sacrificial offering, a service to God, the King. It's a beautiful picture to witness. David, the son of Jesse, was entrusted with a gift symbolic of the Messiah.

Pick of the Crop: In the family of God, we need to bear in mind our Lord "did not come to be served, but to serve, and to give His life a ransom for many" (Mark 10:45). The washing of the disciples' feet was a tutorial for those of us who would follow in their footsteps. The suffering servant laid down His life, which germinated in the hearts of His followers, flourishing to the uttermost parts of the world. The life of a servant is a fruitful one that will manifest itself in due season.

120 The Genealogy: The King

David means *the beloved*. He's one of the greatest lovers of God recorded in Scripture. His life in myriad ways pictures the life of Christ. There's only one person given the name David in the Bible, and there's only one name given under heaven whereby mankind is saved, the name of Jesus Christ (Acts 4:12).

- David was the greatest king Israel had ever known. Jesus is the greater King Israel would come to know.
- David was from Bethlehem (1 Samuel 16). Jesus was born in Bethlehem (Matthew 2:1).
- David had a zeal for God (Psalm 69:9). Jesus had a zeal for God (John 2:17).
- David was a shepherd (Psalm 78:70–71). Jesus is the Good Shepherd (John 10:14).
- David was anointed (2 Samuel 5:3). Jesus was anointed (Acts 4:27).
- David was a king (2 Samuel 2:4). Jesus is King of Kings (Revelation 19:16).
- David had the Spirit of the Lord come down upon him (1 Samuel 16:13). Jesus had the Holy Ghost descend upon Him (Luke 3:22).
- David's throne is established forever (2 Samuel 7:16). Jesus' throne is established forever (Hebrews 1:8).
- David was a servant of God (2 Samuel 7:19). Jesus is a servant of God (Isaiah 42:1).
- David spoke of the Holy Ghost (2 Samuel 23:2). Jesus spoke of the Holy Ghost (John 14:16–17).

- David wept over death (2 Samuel 19:1). Jesus wept over death (John 11:35).
- David was betrayed by a friend and counselor (Psalm 41:9). Jesus was betrayed by a friend and disciple (Luke 22:48).
- David was mocked (2 Samuel 16:8). Jesus was mocked (Luke 22:63).
- David crossed the Brook Kidron to safety (2 Samuel 15:23). Jesus crossed the Brook Kidron for solitude (John 18:1).
- David, fleeing death, ascends the Mount of Olives weeping (2 Samuel 15:30). Jesus, facing death, ascends the Mount of Olives in agony (Luke 22:39).
- One of David's men asked for the head of the king's enemy (2 Samuel 16:9). One of Jesus' disciples severed the ear of Christ's enemy (Matthew 26:51).
- David allowed a verbal assault, which fulfilled prophecy (2 Samuel 16:10–11). Jesus allowed His vicious arrest, which fulfilled prophecy (Matthew 26:54–57).
- David prevented bloodshed (2 Samuel 16:10). Jesus healed the blood that was shed (Luke 22:50–51).

David and Jesus died, and yet this comparison of the two kings continues. Jesus had the power to lay down His life and to take it up again (John 10:18). And David? His hope was in God, and David is more alive than you and I today. "He is not the God of the dead, but the God of the living" (Mark 12:27). If you believe King David ceased to exist outside of this world, you too have made a great mistake.

Pick of the Crop: Jesus Christ, the Son of God in the supreme family of God, is the King of righteousness and the King of peace. He is both the King of glory and the King eternal. He is the King of the Jews and the King of Israel. That baby of Bethlehem is the King of kings and the Lord of lords.

121 The Genealogy: The Mercies of God

Naomi and Ruth were noticeably silent at this phase of their development in Bethlehem. No longer agitated by the rudiments of this world, both rested in love united. Boaz's bond with Ruth bore fruit, and Naomi, beholding her grandson, bore witness of the mercies of God.

"An Ammonite or Moabite shall not enter the assembly of the Lord; even to the tenth generation none of his descendants shall enter the assembly of the Lord forever" (Deuteronomy 23:3). It is believed this law applied to men not women as we clearly see here with Ruth, our proselyte, involved among the people of God. Ten generations from Perez, a breach, to David, the beloved, he moved freely within and without the congregation of the Lord. O the mercies of God in the promised seed, for through it the God gene passed down through generations of Old Testament believers and carried into the New Testament.

The pattern of bearing fruit after its own kind was given to us in the beginning (Genesis 1:11). God speaks out, and we look and listen. There's a difference between a heavenly genealogy and an earthly genealogy, a heavenly seed and an earthly seed. God said he'd put enmity between the seed of the woman and the seed of Satan. "He shall bruise your head, and you shall bruise His heel" (Genesis 3:15).

Luke's genealogy traces Christ back to Adam, "the son of God" (Luke 3:23–38), and the seed God promised Abraham was Christ. "Now to Abraham and his Seed were the promises made. He does not say, 'And to seeds,' as of many, but as of one, 'And to your Seed,' who is Christ" (Galatians 3:16). Matthew's account spells it out: "The book of the genealogy of Jesus Christ, the Son of David, the Son of Abraham" (Matthew 1:1; see also Hebrews 2:16; 2 Timothy 2:8).

Hallelujah, the promised Messiah has come! "And the Word became flesh and dwelt among us, and we beheld His glory, the glory as of the only begotten of the Father, full of grace and truth" (John 1:14). The eternal Word of God, the promised Seed, put on the form of a man and walked this earth.

"Now this is the genealogy." Mankind violated the law of God, and a breach surrounded them like a high wall. My kinsman willingly sacrificed an enchanted covering, came swiftly in strength to serve, existing in the Beloved. That was Christ Jesus, and it's the lovely story of redemption, the story within history, nestled in the names of the above genealogy.

"Jesse begot David." Ruth 4:22

It's fitting that the last *word* in this divinely breathed, God-given, glorious book of Ruth seals the book with a banner of the ever-present love of God. Ruth the Moabitess was lovely. She was loved by the Beloved and was a lover of the Beloved. O that the same might be said of us in the closing chapters of our lives.

Pick of the Crop: We find rich mercies in God. Naomi returned to His love and mercy. Ruth discovered His love and mercy, and Boaz extended His love and mercy. If you are lost in Moab—that wash pot (Psalm 60:8)—come home to the sweet love and mercies of God. He is the Father of mercies and a friend of sinners (2 Corinthians 1:3; Matthew 11:19). Only God in Christ Jesus is where you will be forever loved.

In the service of Jesus Christ, the Son of David,
the Son of Abraham, the Son of God.
Amen.

Brother Kevin Foster

About the Author

Kevin Foster is an award winning PA-C, NP, (Graduate of USC School of Medicine) board-certified Physician Assistant and Nurse Practitioner. Before his medical career, he lived in Liberia, West Africa, with a medical missionary doctor who was a student of the Bible and a teacher of God's Word. Kevin also attended the African Bible College (A.B.C.) and had a traveling film ministry.

Kevin has traveled through the United States and sixteen countries as a part of a global skateboard, Bible-teaching ministry, speaking and teaching youth on the importance of loving God and living by the Word of God.

Back in his home town, Kevin and his team started a house Bible study fellowship that continued for over twenty years.

Kevin has a compassionate heart toward his patients after surviving surgery for the removal of a brain tumor and cancer (lymphoma). When he's not practicing medicine, he can be found spending time enjoying his family, preaching, and teaching at churches, Bible studies, and small Deaf groups.

He lives in the United States with his wife and their four children.

Photo Credit: William Culpepper

Photo Design: Byron Foster

CPSIA information can be obtained at www.ICGtesting.com
Printed in the USA
LVOW12s0307190615

442913LV00005B/5/P